MARY NORDEN

Decorative Embroidery

PHOTOGRAPHY BY SANDRA LANE

The Reader's Digest Association, Inc.
Pleasantville, New York/Montreal

**This book is dedicated to Sylvie,
with my love**

A READER'S DIGEST BOOK

Designed and edited by Conran Octopus Limited

The credits and acknowledgments that appear on page 144
are hereby made a part of this copyright page.

Library of Congress Cataloging in Publication Data
Norden, Mary.
    Decorative embroidery : more than 50 creative projects and design
variations for the home / Mary Norden; photography by Sandra Lane.
        p. cm.
    "A Reader's digest book."
    Includes index.
    ISBN 0-89577-933-1
    1. Embroidery—Patterns.   2. House furnishings.   I. Title.
TT771.N58   1997
746.44'041—dc21   96-48235

Commissioning editor **Suzannah Gough**
Project editor **Helen Ridge**
Assistant editor **Tessa Clayton**
Copy editor **Alison Bolus**
Art editor **Alison Barclay**
Illustrator **Carolyn Jenkins**
Stylist **Mary Norden**
Production **Mano Mylvaganam**

Printed in Hong Kong

Contents

I love the way a few simple stitches can transform an uninteresting piece of household linen or the plainest of fabrics into something special and unique—a white pillowcase embroidered with a monogram becomes exclusive, while a blue linen curtain needs no more than a border of simple posies to look exquisite.

Embroidery encompasses many different types of fabric decoration, some so beautiful and detailed that it is difficult to believe that a needle and thread created them. However, it is my aim to show that a design using one or two embroidery stitches can be just as effective, if not more so, as an ambitious piece worked in many stitches. For this book I have limited myself to fifteen elementary stitches and used them in a range of different, but straightforward, projects. Like any craft, embroidery is best learned by starting with the basics—jump too quickly into the deep end and you will almost certainly become disillusioned. But once you have mastered a few easy stitches and embroidered a design successfully, you will have the confidence to tackle more ambitious projects and may even feel inspired to create your own patterns.

Mary Norden

Posies and Sprigs

FOR THE EMBROIDERER, flowers offer an endless source of inspiration. They can be translated into the simplest of garlands or into larger, more intricate bouquets. They can be used singly to embellish the center of a cushion or the corner of a handkerchief, in rows to form exquisite decorative borders for sheets and curtains, or placed at random, reminiscent of simple eighteenth-century sprigged fabrics.

For a more traditional floral pattern, the shape and detail of each flower head will often dictate which stitches to use. The Sprays of Wildflowers design is a good example of this. French knots make perfect flower stamens, while lazy-daisy stitches are ideal for the long, thin petals of the yellow daisies and blue cornflowers. For more abstract flowers and leaves, there is much more scope for experimenting with different stitches.

I have embroidered the eight-petaled Stylized Blooms in four different ways, but there are many other combinations of stitches you can use, and the Delicate Posies design works just as well stitched solidly in satin stitch as it does with each petal outlined in lazy-daisy stitch.

The bold, interesting shapes of leaves translate well into embroidery too. They are at their freshest when outlined with a simple stitch and worked in just one color.

LEFT: Two simple stitches, stem and fern, convey beautifully the essence of a horse chestnut leaf. OPPOSITE: Simple bags made from remnants of raw silk and linen fabric are embroidered with bold stylized flowers in a mixture of creamy colors.

DELICATE POSIES

ABOVE: The flower petals on this chair-back cover needed to be robust to withstand wear and tear, and were embroidered in padded satin stitch. OPPOSITE: The petals on the curtain border were worked in delicate lazy-daisy stitch, giving a light and airy feel.

Posies, like bouquets, have been a constant theme in fabric design, from the smallest, daintiest bunches to larger arrangements that combine a variety of flowers. Refreshingly simple and unpretentious, they evoke images of romance, gift-giving, and the sentiments of spring and summer.

The posy design shown here, embroidered singly on the chair-back covers and repeated to form a border on the curtain, uses a simple palette of colors that gives it a fresh appeal. In addition to variations in the scale and positioning of the posies, different effects are easy to achieve simply by varying the embroidery stitches.

MATERIALS

- DMC stranded embroidery cotton in the following colors:

    cream 712

    pink 3687

    yellow 3822

    green 3347 (*curtain only*)

Quantities for the curtain depend on the length of the border to be worked. One skein of cream is enough for three complete posies. One skein of each of the other three colors will embroider as many as six posies.

I used cream to embroider all three chair-back covers. For the green and yellow covers I worked the center of the flowers in pink; for the pink cover I substituted yellow. For one posy enlarged to 8in (20cm) tall I used two skeins of cream and half a skein at most of pink or yellow.

For the curtain

- enough plain blue linen to finish one or two curtains to the required size

For the chair-back cover(s)

- 20 x 36in (50 x 90cm) of colored cotton or linen fabric for each cover, or ready-made chair-back covers to fit your chairs
- 15 x 17in (38 x 43cm) thin foam pad(s), or the correct size required to fit ready-made chair-back covers
- 16in (40cm) of 1in (2.5cm) wide cream cotton ties for each cover

For all projects

- tracing paper
- crewel (embroidery) needle size 6
- dressmaker's carbon paper
- embroidery hoop

STITCHES USED

French knot

stem stitch

straight stitch (*curtain only*)

lazy-daisy stitch (*curtain only*)

padded satin stitch (*chair-back cover only*)

For full details on stitches, see pages 132–7.

TECHNIQUES

For full practical information on the methods used in this project, refer to Techniques on pages 129–31.

TEMPLATE

you will need 4in (10cm) for the heading and 4–8in (10–20cm) for the hem, depending on how deep you want it to be.

All the flower heads are worked with three strands of thread, and the stems are worked with six strands. Start by stitching the flower heads, using cream thread and working each petal in lazy-daisy stitch. With pink thread, work one small straight stitch at the top of each petal to cover the securing stitch (see illustration below). In the center of each flower head, work three or four French knots in yellow. Finally, work the green stems in stem stitch.

If you are embroidering a pair of curtains, reverse the pattern on the second curtain so that both sets of posies lean toward each other. To do this, turn the template over to give a mirror image. The template is suitable for a right-hand curtain; the photograph opposite shows the design on a left-hand curtain.

RIGHT: After working each petal in lazy-daisy stitch, color each petal tip with one small straight stitch in pink. Bring the needle through to the right side at the tip of the petal and insert it inside so the colored thread covers the stitch holding down the loop of the lazy-daisy stitch.

To work the curtain

Trace the template above using the tracing paper or, if you want a larger posy, enlarge the template to the required size on a photocopier. Using a tape measure and straight pins, plan the placement of the posies along the edge of the curtain fabric. I positioned each of my posy motifs 3½in (9cm) apart (measuring from the top of one motif to the bottom of the stems of the next), and 2in (5cm) from the outer edge. This latter measurement included a 1in (2.5cm) side hem allowance for finishing the curtains. For a denser border pattern, position the flowers closer together. Use dressmaker's carbon paper to transfer the pattern. Do not extend the border too near the bottom or the top of the curtain;

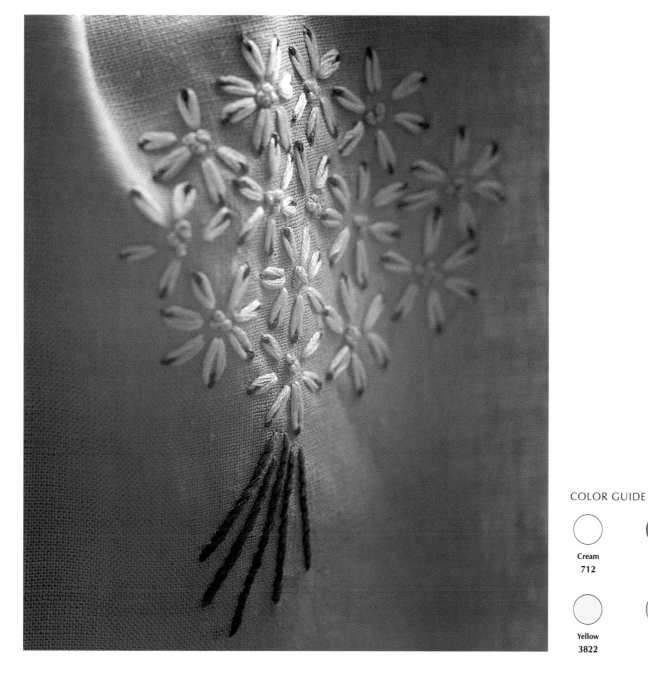

COLOR GUIDE

Cream
712

Pink
3687

Yellow
3822

Green
3347

To finish the curtain

Finish the curtain(s) as required (depending on your choice of heading), using the hem and heading allowances. It is a good idea to line the curtain to protect the back of the embroidery.

To work the chair-back cover

If you are making your own cover, measure two pieces of fabric, each 15 x 17in (38 x 43cm). Add a ¾in (2cm) seam allowance all around, then cut out. Put one piece aside for backing.

Enlarge the posy template on page 14 to 180% on a photocopier. Using dressmaker's carbon paper, transfer the pattern onto the fabric. The best way to get the correct position is to fold the cover lengthwise over the chair it is intended for, or to fold the fabric in half, then position the posy carefully in the center of one half.

The flower petals are worked using three strands of thread and the flower centers and stems with six strands. Start by stitching the petals in padded satin stitch (referring to the template for the direction in which the stitches should run). In the center of each flower work several French knots in pink or yellow to form a neat clump. For each stem work two rows of stem stitch in cream, narrowing to one row at the top to give a tapered effect.

To finish the chair-back cover

Cut the ties into four equal parts. Position the pieces on top of the right side of the backing fabric, two on either side, 2½in (6cm) from the top and bottom edges (this includes the seam allowance). The ties should be facing inward. Sew securely ¾in (2cm) from the side edges. Place the embroidered piece and the backing fabric right sides together (making sure the ties are inside) and pin. Sew together with a ¾in (2cm) seam, leaving a large enough opening for the foam pad. Turn to the right side, and press before inserting the pad. Close the opening with back or running stitch. Tie the ties into bows.

Three beautifully embroidered chair-back covers set the mood for a leisurely summer meal. If you prefer to use fabric in just one shade, vary the color of each posy.

GARLANDS OF FLOWERS

A simple pattern of pink flowers linked by delicate curving stems gives starched sheets and pillowcases a romantic touch. This set of bed linen illustrates how four different border patterns can be achieved from just one design, either by varying the type of stitch used or by working only part of the template. The design would work equally well as a border for curtains or a tablecloth, or singly on buttons, as well as in numerous different color schemes, from the palest of pastels to darker shades of blue.

MATERIALS

- DMC stranded embroidery cotton in the following colors:
    - pink 3607
    - red 606
    - green 704

    For the single sheet, one skein of each color is sufficient. For a double, queen-, or king-size sheet, you will need a second skein of green and pink.
- plain cotton or linen sheet and pillowcases or, if you prefer to make your own, cotton sheeting
- small remnants of fine cotton or linen for buttons
- button-covering kits—these vary in size from ½–1½in (11–38mm) in diameter. I used sizes ⅞in and 1³⁄₁₆in (22mm and 29mm).
- tracing paper
- crewel (embroidery) needle size 6
- dressmaker's carbon paper
- embroidery hoop

STITCHES USED

For items embroidered with outlined flowers
- back stitch
- straight stitch
- French knot
- fern stitch

For items embroidered with solid flowers
- satin stitch
- French knot
- chain stitch

For full details on stitches, see pages 132–7.

TECHNIQUES

For full practical information, see pages 129–31.

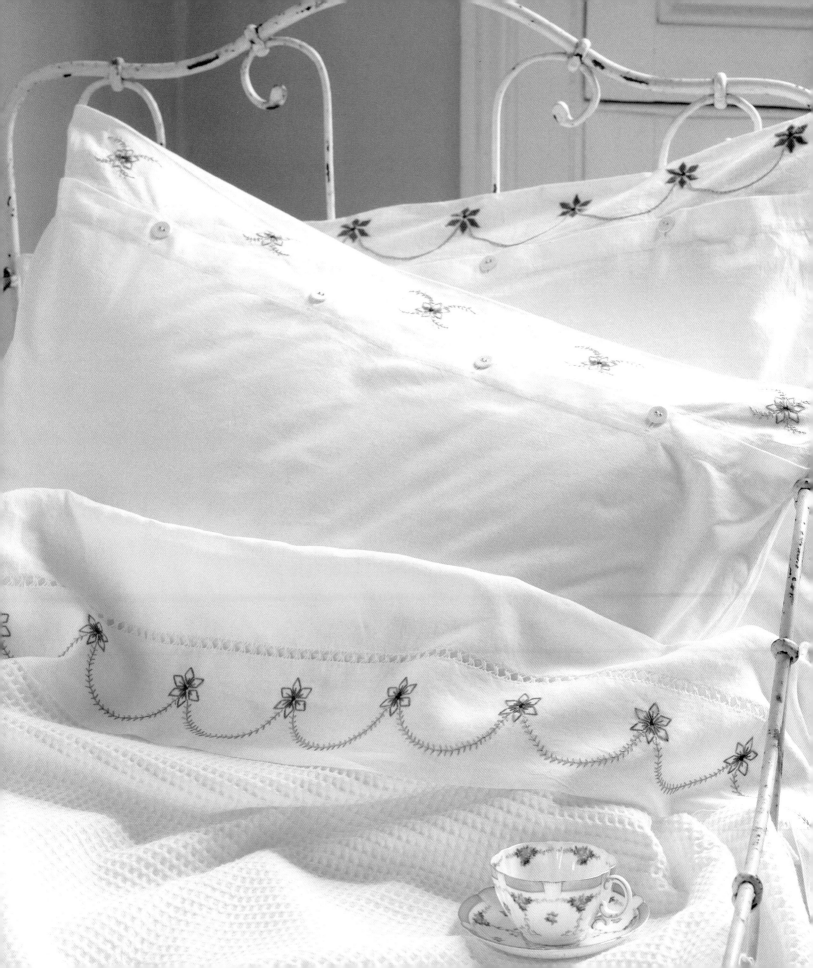

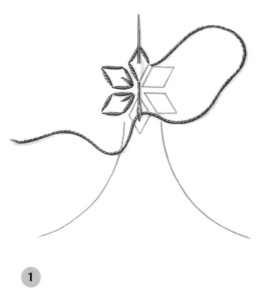

1. To embroider the flowers for the sheet, first outline each petal with four large back stitches, finishing with one straight stitch in the center.
2. Embroider each scallop in fern stitch.

1

2

To work the sheet with outlined flowers
Enlarge the template opposite to 125% on a photo-copier. Using dressmaker's carbon paper, transfer the template onto your sheet as instructed below.

Place the first flower in the center of the top edge of the sheet, and continue to repeat the flower and scallop motif on either side of this first flower, working out toward both side edges of the sheet. This will ensure that the border pattern finishes symmetrically at the sheet edges.

The entire design is worked with three strands of thread. First, stitch the petals in pink, starting at the center point of each one. Outline each petal with four large back stitches, and then work one straight stitch in the center of each petal (see 1 above). In the center of each flower, embroider three French knots in red. Following the line of the scallop, work fern stitch from one flower to the next in green (see 2 above and top right of photograph opposite).

To work the pillowcase with outlined flowers
Enlarge the flower head only of the template oppos-ite to 110% on a photocopier. Using a tape measure and straight pins, plan the placement of the flower heads along the edge of the pillowcase. I positioned each of my motifs 6in (15cm) apart. For a denser pattern, position the flowers closer together. Using dressmaker's carbon paper, transfer the template to your pillowcase. Stitch the flowers as for the sheet.

To create the curling stems (see top left of photo-graph opposite), draw freehand with a pencil a short curve on either side of each flower, or, if it helps, trace around something of a suitable size. Work the stems in fern stitch as for the sheet.

To work the pillowcase with solid flowers
Following the instructions for the sheet border, transfer the template opposite along the edge of the pillowcase.

The flower petals and the scallop are worked with three strands of thread, and the French knots with six. Embroider the petals in satin stitch, working the stitches horizontally (see center of the photograph on the right). In the center of each flower, work just one French knot. Finally, following the line of the scallop, work chain stitch from one flower to the next.

To work the buttons (outlined and solid)

Enlarge or reduce the flower head of the template below to fit the button to be covered. Using dressmaker's carbon paper, transfer the template several times onto the fabric pieces, depending on the number of buttons to be covered. Leave a suitable gap between the motifs to allow for cutting out.

Stitch the outlined flowers as for the sheet, or the solid flowers as for the second pillowcase. If you are using very small buttons, reduce the number of strands to two, or even one.

Finish the buttons according to the instructions given with the button-covering kit.

TEMPLATE

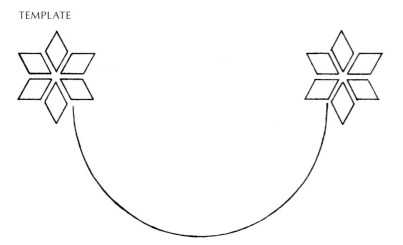

COLOR GUIDE

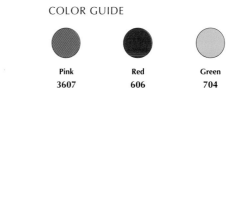

Pink	Red	Green
3607	606	704

SCATTERED LEAVES

This design is made up of three different leaf motifs —oak, maple, and horse chestnut—all chosen for their strong and interesting shapes. I have used bright shades in the ever-popular combinations of blue and white and green and white, which give a feeling of freshness and are reminiscent of spring. For the tablecloth the leaves are scattered across the fabric in a very informal way, but they would look equally effective arranged in a row along the edges of the tablecloth to form a border pattern. For a more abstract effect, each leaf design could be dramatically enlarged to fill the front of a cushion cover. In this case, six strands of embroidery thread, rather than the three required for the tablecloth, would be needed.

BELOW: The corner of a colored napkin is embellished with two oak leaves. In contrast to those on the tablecloth, these leaves are finely detailed, with extra veins and stems.

MATERIALS

- DMC stranded cotton in the following colors:
    - fresh green 704
    - lime green 3819
    - turquoise 913
    - cream 712 (*colored napkins only*)

  Quantities depend on the size of the tablecloth and how densely scattered you want the leaves to be. For my 36in (90cm) square cloth with 15 leaves (five each of the three different shapes), one skein of each color was sufficient. One extra skein of fresh green was required to embroider the border pattern.
- plain cotton or linen tablecloth or, if you prefer to make your own, cotton or linen fabric
- napkins or fabric to match the tablecloth
- crewel (embroidery) needle size 6
- dressmaker's carbon paper
- embroidery hoop

STITCHES USED

fern stitch

back stitch

stem stitch

blanket stitch

straight stitch

chain stitch

For full details on stitches, see pages 132–7.

TECHNIQUES

For full practical information on methods used in this project, see pages 129–31.

LEFT: A plain linen tablecloth is transformed into something exclusive, as well as personal, when embroidered with a few scattered leaves and a simple zig-zag border.

TEMPLATES

MAPLE LEAF

Using fresh green and starting at the top of the stem, embroider blanket stitch around the outline of the maple leaf. The rest of the leaf is worked in stem stitch—single rows for the leaf veins and a double row for the stem.

OAK LEAF

Using turquoise, embroider the center vein of the leaf in back stitch. After every few stitches, work a pair of straight stitches at an angle to create the side veins, which should correspond with the protruding parts of the leaf (see 1 below). Complete the oak leaf by working the outline in chain stitch.

When all the leaves are embroidered, work a zig-zag row of straight stitches along the edge of the tablecloth in fresh green (see 2 opposite).

To work the tablecloth

On a photocopier, enlarge the oak leaf template to 120%, the horse chestnut leaf to 200% and the maple leaf to 135%. Make several copies of each, and cut around them to get rid of the excess paper. Lay the tablecloth flat on the floor, or drape it over the table it is intended for, and scatter the copies over it. When you are satisfied with the arrangement, pin the copies temporarily in place to mark their position. Transfer the leaves onto their marked positions on the fabric, using dressmaker's carbon paper.

The entire design is worked with three strands of thread. Embroider each leaf as follows.

HORSE CHESTNUT LEAF

Using lime green, work fern stitch for the veins of the horse chestnut leaf. Start at the top of each leaf segment with one back stitch and then continue down toward the center, enlarging the stitch as the segment widens and then reducing it as the segment narrows (see photograph opposite). When it becomes too narrow at the center of the leaf to work fern stitch, finish with one or two back stitches. Outline each of the leaves in stem stitch and then finish the design with two rows of stem stitch for each leaf stem.

1. Back stitch is used to create the central vein of the oak leaf, with angled straight stitches for the side veins.
2. A zig-zag line of straight stitches along the edge of the tablecloth shows another way of using this simple stitch.

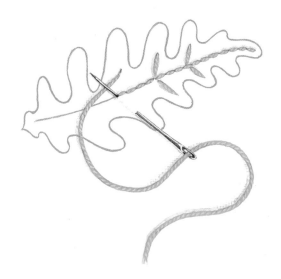

1

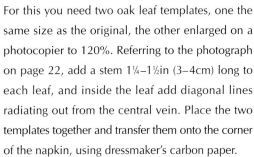

COLOR GUIDE

Fresh green
704

Lime green
3819

Turquoise
913

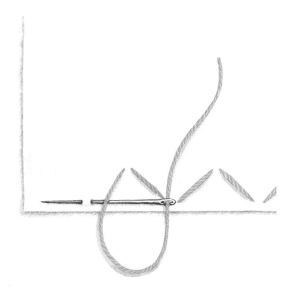

2

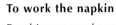

To work the napkin

For this you need two oak leaf templates, one the same size as the original, the other enlarged on a photocopier to 120%. Referring to the photograph on page 22, add a stem 1¼–1½in (3–4cm) long to each leaf, and inside the leaf add diagonal lines radiating out from the central vein. Place the two templates together and transfer them onto the corner of the napkin, using dressmaker's carbon paper.

The entire design is worked with three strands of thread. Using either cream embroidery thread on a colored napkin or one of the green threads on a white napkin, work stem stitch along the diagonal leaf veins. Embroider chain stitch down the center of each leaf and on down the stem. Finally, complete the leaf outlines, still working in chain stitch.

SUMMER SPRIGS

Sprigs are dainty single flowers, each with a short stem and one or two leaves. Traditionally, they were printed onto fabrics in irregular patterns, as though strewn across the cloth. These demure fabrics, known as sprigged cottons, were immensely popular for summer dresses throughout the eighteenth and nineteenth centuries.

My sprigged pillowcase is an homage to these fabrics, informal yet feminine. By contrast, the crisp linen handkerchief features just one sprig, revealed in all its delicate beauty.

MATERIALS

- DMC stranded embroidery cotton in the following colors:
  - deep pink 309
  - yellow 3820
  - pale pink 3779
  - medium pink 335
  - leaf green 470
  - olive green 3051

For the pillowcase, one skein of each color is sufficient. For the handkerchiefs, one skein of each color will work 10 or more sprigs.

For the square pillowcase

- 27½ x 56in (70 x 140cm) square of white cotton or linen fabric, or ready-made square pillowcase
- 22in (55cm) square pillow
- 2¼yd (2.3m) lace trimming
- 12in (30cm) ribbon

ABOVE: A plain white linen handkerchief is the perfect foil for a single dainty sprig in full bloom.
OPPOSITE: The same sprig enlarged and randomly scattered over a prettily trimmed square pillowcase.

For the handkerchief

- ready-made fine white handkerchief or, if you prefer to make your own, fine cotton fabric

For both projects

- triangle
- tracing paper
- crewel (embroidery) needle size 6 for the pillowcase, 9 for the handkerchief
- dressmaker's carbon paper
- embroidery hoop

STITCHES USED

satin stitch
French knot
stem stitch
straight stitch

For full details on stitches, see pages 132–7.

TECHNIQUES

For full practical information, see pages 129–31.

To work the pillowcase

If you are making your own pillowcase, use a triangle and a ruler to measure a 22in (55cm) square on the cotton or linen fabric. Add a 1in (2.5cm) seam allowance all around and cut out.

Trace or photocopy the template 12 times (some of these could be reversed). Cut around these copies very roughly (to get rid of excess paper) and space them evenly across the fabric square or pillowcase. Be careful not to place the sprigs too near the edge

of the fabric, as they might get taken up into the seam. To prevent the design from looking too rigid and regular, alter the angle of each flower sprig so that they are pointing in different directions (refer to the photograph on page 27). Once you are satisfied with the arrangement of your flowers, transfer them onto the fabric or pillowcase using dressmaker's carbon paper.

The entire design is worked with three strands of thread. Refer to the template below for the direction in which the stitches should run. The heavier lines indicate stem stitch. Start by stitching the center of the flower (the area surrounding the yellow stamens) in deep pink, using radiating satin stitch. To achieve an even effect, it helps to work a few straight or guide stitches first (see illustration top right). Next, work a cluster of yellow French knots in the center of each flower to form the stamens.

Work the petals in satin stitch, embroidering two petals in pale pink and the rest in medium pink. If you wish, vary the arrangement of the darker and paler pinks to prevent the flowers from looking unnaturally identical.

Work the hatched area of each leaf in satin stitch, and the leaf outlines in stem stitch. Finally, work the stems with two rows of stem stitch, one slightly shorter than the other to give a tapered effect.

To finish the pillowcase
For the backing, measure two rectangles on the remaining fabric, one 16 x 22in (40 x 55cm) and the other 6 x 22in (15 x 55cm). Add a 1in (2.5cm) seam allowance all around and cut out. Place the two pieces right sides and long edges together and,

using a sewing machine or small back stitches, join along one long edge with a 1in (2.5cm) seam, leaving enough seam open in the middle to insert the pillow. Press the seam open.

With right sides facing, pin and stitch the embroidery to the backing fabric, using a 1in (2.5cm) seam. Snip across the corners to reduce bulk, and turn the case right side out. Sew the lace edging all around the pillowcase, slip stitching along the seam edge. To close the opening at the back, cut the ribbon in two, and sew one length on each side to tie in a bow after the pillow has been inserted.

To work the handkerchief
Reduce the template (left) to 85% on a photocopier. Using dressmaker's carbon paper, transfer the design onto the corner of the handkerchief.

The entire design is worked with two strands of thread. Following the embroidery instructions for the pillowcase, work in exactly the same way.

TEMPLATE

COLOR GUIDE

Deep pink
309

Yellow
3820

Pale pink
3779

Medium pink
335

Leaf green
470

Olive green
3051

STYLIZED BLOOMS

ABOVE: A cushion cover is divided into a grid with lines of chain stitch; each alternate square is filled with a bloom.
OPPOSITE: A single button embellishes an embroidered bloom on a simple bag.

While the petals and leaves of small flowers are well suited to dense stitching, such as the Summer Sprigs embroidered in satin stitch (see page 26), bold, stylized flowers are too large for solid blocks of color. They tend to work better with open stitching and patterns, where plenty of background fabric is visible. This eight-petaled bloom can be worked in four different ways, and can be used either on small bags or in a grid pattern on a cushion cover. If you like, you could add extra textural detail by sewing a button in the center of each bloom.

The projects shown here illustrate how the appearance of one basic motif can vary depending on the type of stitches used and the way in which they are arranged.

MATERIALS

- DMC stranded embroidery cotton in the following colors:
  cream 712 (*fly stitch bag, French knot bag and cushion cover only*)
  toffee 436 (*chain stitch bag only*)
  beige 738 (*French knot bag only*)
- DMC Pearl Cotton No. 5 in cream 712 (*blanket stitch bag only*)
  One skein of thread is more than enough to complete one bloom for a bag. Three skeins are sufficient for the whole cushion.

For the bags
- 20in (50cm) square of linen or cotton fabric for each bag

For the blanket stitch bag, which is embroidered with a thicker thread, it is important to choose a loose-woven fabric that will allow the needle and thread to pass through easily.

For the cushion cover
- 20in (50cm) square of unbleached loose-woven linen fabric, or ready-made cushion cover
- triangle
- tailor's chalk
- tracing paper
- 14in (35cm) zipper
- 16in (40cm) square cushion pad
- 20in (50cm) square of linen for backing

For all projects
- crewel (embroidery) needle size 5
- dressmaker's carbon paper
- embroidery hoop

STITCHES USED

blanket stitch	chain stitch
fly stitch	French knot
stem stitch	

(The blanket stitch and chain stitch bags use just one stitch each, while the French knot and fly stitch bags also use stem stitch. The cushion uses all the stitches.)
For full details on stitches, see pages 132–7.

TECHNIQUES

For full information, see pages 129–31.

1. Blanket stitch bag:
As you work out from the
center of the bloom in blanket
stitch, graduate the stitches to
follow the curve of the petal.
The inner line dictates the
length of each stitch.
2. Chain stitch bag:
Outline all the petals before
working a circle of chain
stitch in the center. To give a
neat finish these stitches
should slightly overlap
the ends of the petal lines.

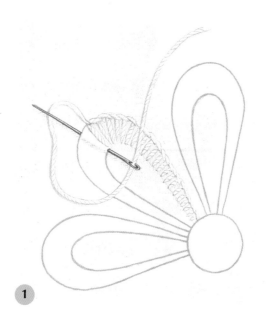

1

To work the chain stitch bag

Enlarge the bloom template on page 34 to 140% on a photocopier. Using dressmaker's carbon paper, transfer the design onto the fabric (see blanket stitch bag for positioning).

The entire design is worked in chain stitch with six strands of thread for the outer edge of the petals and the center and three strands for the inner edge of the petals. Begin stitching each petal at the center, following the pattern lines up, round, and back again to the center. Use larger stitches for the outer edge and the center.

When all the petals are complete, work a circle of chain stitch in the center of the flower, just touching the base of each petal (see 2 below).

To work the blanket stitch bag

Enlarge the bloom template on page 34 to 140% on a photocopier. Using dressmaker's carbon paper, transfer the design onto one of the squares of linen fabric. I positioned my bloom so that the center lay 5½in (14cm) from the bottom of the square and equidistant from both sides. This ensures the correct placement when the bag is made up.

The entire design is embroidered in blanket stitch with six strands of thread. Working from left to right and beginning each petal at the center, start stitching, following the two working lines around and back to the center. As the distance between these two lines widens to mark the thickening of the petals, so you will need to increase the length of the stitches (see 1 above).

When all the petals are complete, work a circle of blanket stitch in the center of the flower.

2

To work the French knot bag

Enlarge the bloom template on page 34 to 140% on a photocopier. Using dressmaker's carbon paper, transfer the design onto the fabric (see blanket stitch bag for positioning).

Unless stated otherwise, six strands of thread are used. First work the outer edge of each petal in stem stitch with cream thread. To give this line a thicker, twisted effect, pass the needle either side of the working line. Now work the inner pattern line of each petal, but this time using only three strands of thread. Continue to work in stem stitch, but this time pass the needle directly along the working line to achieve a finer line. Work two circles of stem stitch in the center of the flower, leaving a gap between

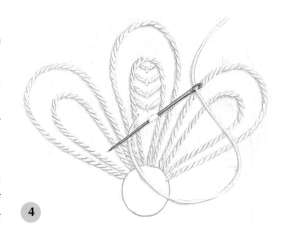

them (see 3 below). Work a row of French knots in beige between the two lines that form the petals and between the two center circles of the flower.

To work the fly stitch bag

Enlarge the bloom template on page 34 to 140% on a photocopier. Using dressmaker's carbon paper, transfer the design onto the fabric (see blanket stitch bag for positioning).

The entire design is worked with six strands of thread. Work both outline edges of each petal in stem stitch. In the center of each petal work a row of seven or eight fly stitches (see 4 above). Finish the flower with a circle of stem stitch in the center.

To finish the bags

For each bag, fold the fabric square in half, right sides together, so that the fold line passes vertically through the embroidery. Machine stitch a ¾in (2cm) seam down the long side. Press the seam, then flatten the bag so that the seam lies in the center of the back. Now stitch a ¾in (2cm) seam along the

3. French knot bag:
To achieve neat circles in the center of the bloom, keep the stem stitches even in length and sloped at exactly the same angle to the line. This way the stitches of the inner circle will be smaller than those of the outer circle.
4. Fly stitch bag:
Work a series of fly stitches, one below the other, down the center of each petal. As the petal lines narrow, reduce the size of each stitch, but not the distance between them.

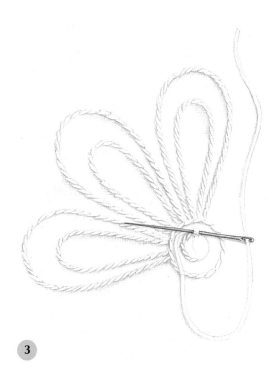

bottom of the bag and a ¾in (2cm) hem around the top. Turn the bag right side out. Fold the top 5in (12.5cm) to the inside and sew a row of top stitching around the top edge.

To work the cushion cover

Using a triangle and a ruler mark out a 16in (40cm) square on your loose-woven linen. Add on a 1¾in (4.5cm) seam and border allowance all around, then cut out. With tailor's chalk, draw three vertical and three horizontal lines within the marked-out

TEMPLATE

square at 4, 8 and 12in (10, 20 and 30cm), thus dividing it into four rows of 4in (10cm) squares (refer to photograph left). Trace or photocopy the bloom template and transfer it using dressmaker's carbon paper into every alternate square marked out on the fabric. This will give you eight blooms.

The entire design is worked with three strands of thread. Stitch the blooms as for the four bags, working each variation twice. Note that the French knot design has been simplified to suit the smaller scale: it now has only one center circle. Work the dividing grid lines in chain stitch.

To finish the cushion cover

For the backing fabric you will need to cut two pieces of matching linen, one measuring 7¼ x 19½in (18 x 49cm) and the other 13¾ x 19½in (35 x 49cm). Place the two pieces right sides together and with their long sides aligning. Using a sewing machine or small back stitches, join along the long edge with a ¾in (2cm) seam to form a 19½in (49cm) square. Make sure you leave enough seam open in the middle to accommodate the length of the zipper. Press the seams flat. Pin, baste and then machine stitch the zipper into position.

With right sides facing (and the zipper open), pin and machine stitch the embroidered linen square to the backing linen, leaving a 1in (2.5cm) seam allowance all round. Snip across the corners to avoid a bulky finish and turn the cushion cover right side out. Press. Machine stitch a ¾in (2cm) border all around through both layers of fabric. Over this machine line work a line of chain stitch in order to create a frame for the design.

COLOR GUIDE

Toffee
436

SPRAYS OF WILDFLOWERS

BELOW AND OPPOSITE:
A colorful spray of wildflowers
adds the prettiest of touches to
a plain cushion and tray cloth.

Unlike a bouquet of flowers, which tends to be a rather formal arrangement, a spray is more natural, as though the flowers have been effortlessly bunched together. For my spray design I chose to use wild- *flowers, grasses, and long stems for a summery, rustic look, and positioned the designs so that the flowers seem to spill casually over the front of a cushion and the corner of a tray cloth.*

MATERIALS

- DMC stranded embroidery cotton in the following colors for both projects:

    navy 791

    dark purple 553

    medium purple 554

    deep pink 3805

    medium pink 3607

    pale pink 3608

    yellow ochre 3821

    green 471

    Additional colors for the cushion cover:

    cream 3823

    pale purple 210

    orange 350

    bright yellow 743

    apple green 989

    dark lilac 3746

    medium lilac 340

    One skein of each color is more than enough for both the cushion cover and tray cloth.

For the cushion cover
- 20 x 40in (50cm x 1m) of plain cotton or linen fabric, or a ready-made cushion cover
- 12in (30cm) zipper
- 14in (35cm) cushion pad

*RIGHT: As you embroider
long-and-short stitch around
the outside edge of the flower,
use the dotted line as a guide
for the length of the short
stitches. These should extend
from the outside edge to just
over the dotted line. The
alternating long stitches should
be roughly twice the length.*

For the tray cloth
- 20in (50cm) of plain cotton or linen, or a ready-made tray cloth

For both projects
- tracing paper
- triangle
- crewel (embroidery) needle size 6
- dressmaker's carbon paper
- embroidery hoop

STITCHES USED

long-and-short stitch

stem stitch

French knot

straight stitch

lazy-daisy stitch

satin stitch

For full details on stitches, see pages 132–7.

TEMPLATE

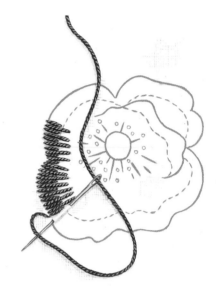

TECHNIQUES

For full information, see pages 129–31.

To work the cushion cover

Using a triangle and a ruler, measure a 16in (40cm) square on your cotton or linen fabric. Add a ¾in (2in) seam allowance all around and cut out. Enlarge the large template opposite to 220% on a photo-copier. Using dressmaker's carbon paper, transfer the design onto the fabric, making sure the pattern is placed in the center of the fabric square.

Refer to the photograph on page 41 for use of color. Start stitching in the center, working the largest flower first. Embroider long-and-short stitch around the whole outside edge and part of the inside of the flower, using the dotted line as a guide for the length of the short stitches (see illustration above). Use stem stitch to outline the outer edges of the long-and-short stitch; this will help to define the shape. Work a

RIGHT: A tumbling mass of
brightly colored wildflowers
will enhance the plainest of
cushion covers. In keeping
with the informality of the
design, the six embroidery
stitches used are easy
and simple.

To finish the cushion cover

For the backing fabric, you will need to measure two pieces of matching fabric, one piece 6 x 16in (15 x 40cm) and the other 10 x 16in (25 x 40cm). Add a ¾in (2cm) seam allowance all around and cut out. Place the two pieces together and, using a sewing machine or small back stitches, join along one long edge with a ¾in (2cm) seam, leaving enough seam open in the middle for the length of the zipper. Press the seam flat. Pin, baste, and then machine stitch the zipper into position.

With right sides facing and zipper open, pin and machine stitch the embroidery to the backing fabric, allowing a ¾in (2cm) seam all round. Snip across the corners to avoid a bulky finish, and turn the cushion cover to the right side. Press. Machine stitch a ½in (1.5cm) border all around through both layers of fabric. Insert the cushion pad.

central clump of French knots, then around these work more French knots, but this time scattered, and with some radiating straight stitches.

The petals of the remaining flowers are worked in lazy-daisy stitch. For the smallest flowers, which are randomly colored in three shades of purple, work one lazy-daisy stitch for each petal and one French knot in the center. The whole cornflowers are also randomly colored, this time in two shades of lilac. Work three lazy-daisy stitches for each petal and, in the center of the flowers, a few French knots. For the daisies work one lazy-daisy stitch for each petal and some French knots in the center.

Work the stems in stem stitch, the sprays of grass in lazy-daisy, and the blades of grass in satin stitch.

To work the tray cloth

The wildflower spray for the tray cloth is made up of just a few elements taken from the whole cushion design. Either use the small template on page 38 or, working freehand or using tracing paper, compose a simple arrangement of flowers and leaves, taking the shapes from the large template on page 39. Using dressmaker's carbon paper, transfer the finished pattern onto one corner of the tray cloth. Be careful not to place the motif too near the edge of the cloth, or you will not be able to mount the fabric into the embroidery hoop.

Color and stitch the design exactly as for the cushion cover. Repeat on the opposite corner of the tray cloth.

COLOR GUIDE

Medium pink	Deep pink	Pale pink	Yellow ochre	Navy	Pale purple	Medium purple	Dark purple
3607	3805	3608	3821	791	210	554	553

Medium lilac	Dark lilac	Orange	Bright yellow	Cream	Green	Apple green
340	3746	350	743	3823	471	989

Nature's Harvest

WHEN I WAS LOOKING FOR images to translate into embroidery for this book, it was often the shape of an object or a flower that inspired me. With the emphasis on the outline of an image, rather than on the finer detail or coloring, stitches could be used quite sparingly—a simple line of chain stitch was enough to convey the elegance of a water jug, while one lazy-daisy stitch made the perfect petal. Sometimes, as in the case of two of the projects in this chapter, richness of color was the inspiration. The irregular outlines of summer fruits and vegetables, such as lemons, strawberries, peas and carrots, are filled and shaded in with solid color and stitches, in the same way that an artist uses a pencil and brush to draw and paint. Working in this way gives enormous scope for playing with different stitches, as almost any embroidery stitch can be adapted for use as a filling stitch. I chose long-and-short stitch, the classic stitch for shading, because I love the way the stitches blend into one another to give a beautifully smooth and solid field of color. If the idea of so many stitches appears daunting, particularly if the motif is to be repeated in a row to form a decorative band, the motif can simply be outlined, as demonstrated by the cherries on the picnic cutlery holder on the right.

LEFT: Cherry motifs are arranged in an orderly pattern along the edge of a cutlery bag.
OPPOSITE: Golden wheat sheaves tumble over a linen basket cloth.

BREAKFAST COCKEREL

The cockerel napkin is an excellent project for the embroidery novice to tackle. It introduces three of the most widely used stitches: stem, satin, and French knot. In addition, the cockerel has been pared down to the simplest of outlines, with just enough detail to give it interest. For the delightful curtain border, where the cockerel is used to form a repeating pattern, no extra skills are required—only more time.

MATERIALS

- DMC stranded embroidery cotton in the following colors:
    - blue 798
    - red 666
    - yellow 973
    - cream 3823 (*blue napkin only*)

    One skein of each color is enough to embroider six napkins. The curtain with six cockerels requires two skeins of blue and one each of yellow and red.
- fine cotton or linen napkins
- ready-made cream cotton or linen curtains, or loose-woven cream linen sufficient to finish a curtain to the required size
- crewel (embroidery) needle size 7 for the napkin, size 5 for the curtain
- dressmaker's carbon paper
- embroidery hoop

STITCHES USED

stem stitch
satin stitch
French knot
straight stitch (*napkins only*)
fly stitch (*curtain border only*)

For full details on stitches, see pages 132–7.

TEMPLATE

TECHNIQUES

For full practical information on the methods used in this project, see pages 129–31.

To work the napkins

Enlarge the template above to 120% on a photocopier. Using dressmaker's carbon paper, transfer the template onto the corner of a napkin. Be careful not to place the cockerel too close to the corner of the napkin, or you will not be able to mount it in the embroidery hoop.

The entire design is worked with three strands of thread. Refer to the photograph on page 47 for the colors used. Start by stitching the outline and the body and tail markings of the cockerel in stem stitch (the direction of your stitches is unimportant). Work the comb, beak, and wattle in satin stitch. Work one French knot for the cockerel's eye and three straight stitches for the feet.

To work the curtain border

Enlarge the template above to 185% on a photocopier. Using a tape measure and straight pins, plan the placement of the cockerels along the bottom edge of the curtain fabric. I positioned each of my

motifs at 6in (15cm) intervals, measuring from the feet of one cockerel to the next, and 3in (7.5cm) from the bottom. This latter measurement includes a 2in (5cm) hem allowance for finishing the curtains. For a denser border pattern, position the cockerels closer together. Use dressmaker's carbon paper to transfer the pattern. Do not extend the border too near the edges of the curtain; you will need to leave 2in (5cm) for each side hem.

Stitch the cockerel as for the napkin, but make the following changes: work all stem stitches with six rather than three strands of thread; work the feet of the bird in stem stitch rather than straight stitch, and embroider the eye with three French knots.

To finish the curtain

Turn under double side hems of 1in (2.5cm) and a double bottom hem of 1in (2.5cm) and neatly hand stitch them in place. Work a row of fly stitches along the bottom of the curtain in red, using three strands of thread (see illustration below). Finally, attach the heading tape of your choice to the top of the curtain and draw up the gathering threads to make the required width.

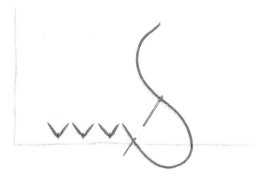

RIGHT: The curtain hem is decorated with fly stitch. Working from left to right, pick up a diagonal stitch, with the needle point over the loop. Then make a small vertical stitch to hold the loop in place.

COLOR GUIDE

Blue
798

Red
666

Yellow
973

GOLDEN WHEAT SHEAVES

Wheat is the ancient symbol of harvest as well as prosperity and fertility and is strongly associated with the countryside and a rural way of life. A field of golden wheat sheaves arranged in shocks is a timeless and evocative scene, and to reinforce this image I chose embroidery threads and fabrics in colors similar to those seen at harvest time—warm shades of gold, yellow, and brown. In keeping with the rustic theme, I embroidered the wheat sheaves randomly over the tablecloth so that they look natural, as though I had no hand in their placement. By contrast, those on the bread basket cloth form a neat border, the sheaves naturally complementing the basket's contents.

RIGHT: A loosely woven linen cloth embroidered with sprays of wheat sheaves adorns a country kitchen table. OPPOSITE: The same design is used to decorate the edge of a bread basket cloth.

MATERIALS

- DMC stranded embroidery cotton in the following colors:
  - gold 783
  - toffee 729
  - sand 676

Quantities depend on the size of tablecloth used and also on the density of pattern. For the 36in (90cm) square cloth with 15 wheat sheaf sprays shown here, two skeins of each color are sufficient. For the border on the bread basket cloth, one skein of each color is plenty.

- natural-colored linen tablecloth or loose-woven natural-colored linen
- basket cloth (I used a very large napkin in fine linen with a drawn-thread border)
- tracing paper
- crewel (embroidery) needle size 5 for the tablecloth, size 7 for the basket cloth
- dressmaker's carbon paper
- embroidery hoop

STITCHES USED

lazy-daisy stitch

stem stitch

running stitch

For full details on stitches, see pages 132–7.

TECHNIQUES

For full practical information on the methods used in this project, refer to Techniques on pages 129–31.

COLOR GUIDE

Gold
783

Toffee
729

Sand
676

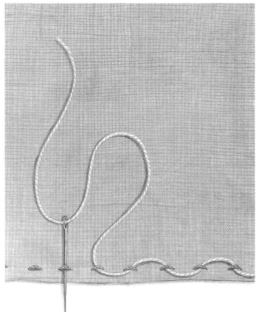

LEFT: To edge the tablecloth hem, first work a line of running stitches. Bring a thread in a contrasting color through at one end of the line, and pass it in and out of the stitches without picking up any fabric. This thread passes through the material only at the beginning and end of its length.

To work the tablecloth

Enlarge the template above to 175% on a photocopier. To help you plan the placement of your pattern, copy this enlarged motif several times. Very roughly cut around these copies to get rid of the excess paper. Lay the tablecloth flat on the floor, or drape it over the table it is intended for, and randomly arrange the copies of the wheat sheaves (refer to the photograph on page 50). When you are satisfied with the arrangement, pin the copies temporarily to mark their position. Using dressmaker's carbon paper, transfer the pattern.

The entire design is worked with six strands of thread. Refer to the photograph on page 51 for the use of color. The ears of wheat are worked in lazy-daisy stitch and their stems in stem stitch. Continue working in stem stitch for the wheat blades, but this time alter the angle so that the needle passes from one side of the blade to the other; this gives a thicker, twisted effect. To widen the blade, increase the angle of the stitches as you work progressively down it.

To decorate the hem of the tablecloth, first embroider a row of well-spaced running stitches along the edge, then weave a contrasting color in and out of these stitches (see illustration above). Be careful not to pull the thread too tight.

To work the bread basket cloth

Trace the template above. Using a tape measure and straight pins, plan the placement of the wheat sheaves along the edge of your bread basket cloth (see photograph opposite). To prevent the design from looking too regular, alter the angle of each motif so that they are pointing in slightly different directions. Work the wheat sheaves as for the tablecloth, but use only three strands of thread instead of six for a finer result.

If your bread basket cloth does not already have a border pattern, you may want to add the same border pattern as the one used for the tablecloth. Or you could use a row of fly stitches like those used for the cockerel curtain border on page 48.

SUMMER FRUIT

These jug covers have each been embroidered with a different summer fruit. The lusciousness of the fruit is emphasized by the rich coloring and the solid stitching—mainly satin stitch. For both decorative and practical reasons, each cover has been trimmed with beads; the weight of these helps to hold the covers down over the jugs.

In contrast, the picnic cutlery holder (below left), decoratively edged with outlined cherries, shows how a design can be adapted. A single cherry has been taken from the template and repeated in a row. To prevent the design from looking too regular, the angle of every alternate cherry is reversed, so the stalks point in opposite directions.

BELOW: Perfect for summer picnics, a canvas cutlery holder is embroidered with a simple row of cherries. Each cherry is outlined and highlighted with stem stitch, while satin stitch completes each stalk.

MATERIALS

- DMC stranded embroidery cotton in the following colors:

  For the strawberry
    bright red 666
    dark red 321
    pink 3705
    cream 712
    pale green 471
    dark green 470

  For the cherries
    scarlet 304
    plum red 815
    dark red 321
    cream 712
    orange 349
    green 471

  For the lemon
    cream 3823
    medium yellow 726
    pale yellow 727

  For all three fruits, one skein of each color will work several jug covers.

- white cotton fabric, enough for an 8¾in (22cm) square for each cover, or to the size of your choice
- small beads (see instructions below for quantities and colors, but do not feel you have to stick to my color scheme)
- triangle
- tracing paper
- crewel (embroidery) needle size 6
- dressmaker's carbon paper
- embroidery hoop

STITCHES USED

satin stitch
long-and-short stitch
straight stitch (*lemon only*)
back stitch (*lemon and cherries only*)
French knot (*strawberry only*)
stem stitch (*cherries only*)
running stitch

For full details on stitches, see pages 132–7.

TECHNIQUES

For full practical information on the methods used in this project, refer to Embroidery Techniques on pages 129–31.

ABOVE AND LEFT: Jugs of cooling summer drinks are draped with beaded covers embroidered with fruits of the season—a strawberry, a lemon, and a bunch of ripe cherries.

1. Working from right to left, embroider a line of long-and-short stitch along the bottom edge of the strawberry and two thirds of the way up the left side. The short stitches must not extend beyond the dotted line, while the long stitches should, ready to blend with the next row of color.

2. Shading with two or more colors: until you have finished a color within a particular area, leave the needle threaded but put to one side.

To work the strawberry

Using a triangle and a ruler, measure an 8in (20cm) square. Add a ¾in (2cm) hem allowance all around and cut out. Trace the strawberry template on page 58, and use dressmaker's carbon paper to transfer it onto the middle of the fabric square.

The entire design is worked with three strands of thread. Work in long-and-short stitch as follows. With bright red, stitch a line of long-and-short stitches along the bottom and up the left side of the strawberry (see 1 above). Work next to these stitches an area in dark red, as indicated by the dotted line on the template and, also in dark red, the dotted area along the top edge. In the oval dotted area to the right, work in pink. Embroider the rest of the strawberry in bright red. When all the long-and-short stitch is completed, work French knots in cream at random over the strawberry, scattering them more sparsely as you work downward (see photograph on page 55). Alternating the use of the two different greens, work the stem and leaves in satin stitch, placing the stitches across the leaf or stem shape.

Hem the cover with running stitch in bright red. Sew one red bead at each corner of the square and nine evenly spaced along each edge.

To work the cherries

Mark and cut out your fabric as for the strawberry cover. Trace the cherry template on page 58, and use dressmaker's carbon paper to transfer it onto the center of the fabric square.

The entire design is worked with three strands of thread. Stitch one cherry at a time, starting with the central cherry and working in long-and-short stitch (see 2 below). Embroider from the bottom upward. Rather than completing one area of color at a time, work back and forth horizontally across each cherry. Use several needles threaded at once, one for each color. When a color or colors are not in use, simply put the needle(s) and thread(s) to one side until required.

The left side edge of the first cherry is worked in scarlet, which blends into an area of plum red, as

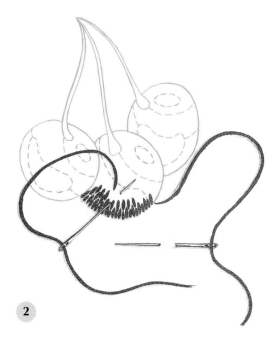

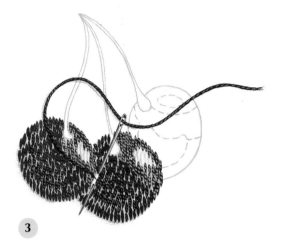

3

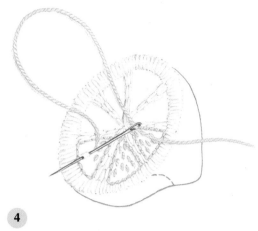

4

3. To help define the outline of the first cherry so it does not blend with the second, work a line of small back stitches along the overlap.
4. For the flesh of each lemon segment, work short straight stitches. Arrange these in lines radiating out from the center.

indicated by the dotted line. Down the center of the cherry is an area of dark red, and to the right, surrounding the small highlight of cream, an area of orange. Shade the left-hand cherry in the same way, working a line of back stitch in plum red along the line where the two cherries overlap (see 3 above). Stitch the remaining cherry, again working a line of back stitch where it meets the central cherry. Embroider the stems in stem stitch, starting at the top of each stem and finishing at the base with a few satin stitches.

Hem the cover with running stitch in bright red. Sew on one green and two red beads at each corner.

To work the lemon

Mark and cut out your fabric as for the strawberry cover. Trace the lemon wedge template on page 58, and use dressmaker's carbon paper to transfer it onto the middle of the fabric square.

The entire design is worked with three strands of thread. Start stitching with cream, working the lemon pith first. Embroider the outer circle of pith in satin stitch, radiating the stitches outward, and then fill the narrow areas of pith between each segment with long and short stitches. Outline each segment with back stitch in medium yellow, then fill each one with short straight stitches (see 4 above). Completely cover the peel of the lemon with long-and-short stitches, working one third in pale yellow and the other two thirds in medium yellow.

Hem the cover with running stitch in medium yellow. Sew one green bead at each corner of the square and four evenly spaced white beads along each of the edges.

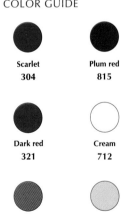

COLOR GUIDE

Scarlet **304**	Plum red **815**
Dark red **321**	Cream **712**
Orange **349**	Green **471**

TEMPLATES

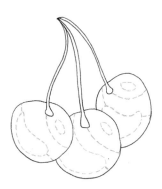

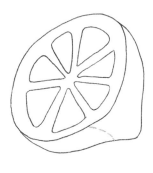

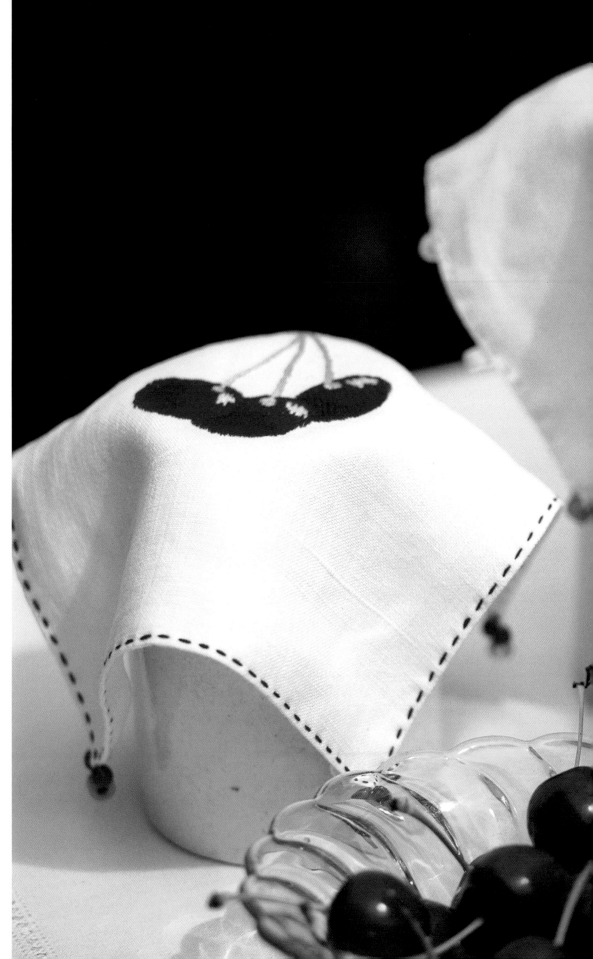

GARDEN VEGETABLES

A few basic embroidery stitches are sometimes all that is necessary to convey the image of a beautiful flower. A vegetable, however, is less delicate in shape and requires more detail to prevent it from looking crude. Both the bunch of carrots and the peapods designs use a palette of natural colors, which is one of the first things you notice about them, along with the density of their stitching. Both images are completely covered in stitches, nearly all of which are long-and-short stitch. This is the most widely used of all close filling stitches, largely because it is so quick and easy, and is ideal for the gradual blending of color. Like shading with colored crayons, it is this subtle blending that gives the embroidered images a three-dimensional effect.

BELOW AND OPPOSITE: A picnic basket is lined with a cloth richly embroidered with a bunch of carrots, while another cloth, decorated with two ripe peapods, holds freshly picked peas. The realistic coloring of both designs is achieved with long-and-short stitch.

MATERIALS

- DMC stranded embroidery cotton in the following colors:

  For the peapods

  dark green 987

  cream 712

  light green 471

  medium green 988

  pale green 472

  For the carrots

  dark green 367

  light green 368

  bright orange 946

  dark orange 720

  medium orange 721

  pale orange 722

  cream 712

  One skein of each color is more than enough for both projects.

- cream cotton or linen tablecloth for each project, or sufficient cotton or linen fabric
- crewel (embroidery) needle size 6
- dressmaker's carbon paper
- embroidery hoop

STITCHES USED

satin stitch

long-and-short stitch

straight stitch

stem stitch

For full details on stitches, see pages 132–7.

TEMPLATE

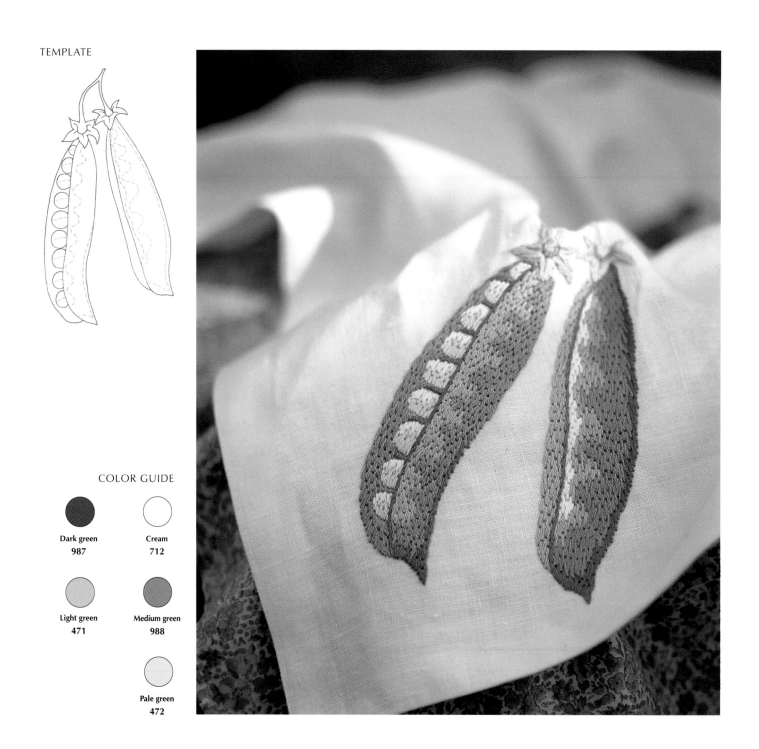

COLOR GUIDE

Dark green
987

Cream
712

Light green
471

Medium green
988

Pale green
472

TECHNIQUES

For full practical information on the methods used in this project, refer to Techniques on pages 129–31.

To work the peapods

Enlarge the peapods template opposite to 200% on a photocopier. Using dressmaker's carbon paper, transfer the design onto one corner of your cloth. Be careful not to place the motif too close to the corner, or you will not be able to mount it in the embroidery hoop.

The entire design is worked with three strands of thread. Refer to the photographs for color and stitch direction. Work the left-hand peapod first. With dark green, embroider a few satin stitches in between each pea (see illustration at right). Now work in long-and-short stitch only. First shade the peas with cream and light green thread. Work the area to the left of the peas in medium green and the area to the right, up to the dotted wavy line, in pale green. At the base of the pod, work a few stitches in dark green before extending this color up the right-hand side of the pod, using the dotted line. Complete the rest of the pod in medium green. Down the center of the motif, along the edge of the peas, work a row of stem stitches in dark green.

Next work the right-hand peapod. Embroider the left side of the pod in pale green. Moving to the right, highlight a small area down the length of the pod in cream, and then stitch in pale green in the area indicated by the dotted lines. At the base of the pod and up its outer edge, work a few stitches in dark green before completing the rest of the pod in medium green. Down the center of the pod, work a row of stem stitches in dark green along the edge of the cream highlight.

With light green thread, stitch the pod stems in satin stitch, making the stitches at a slight angle rather than straight across the stem. Around the base of the stem, embroider the pod tops or leaves in satin stitch, radiating the stitches outward down the length of each leaf. Change to medium green thread, and work one straight stitch in the center of each leaf in the same direction. Finish by embroidering a few tiny stem stitches around the base of the stem to define the shape.

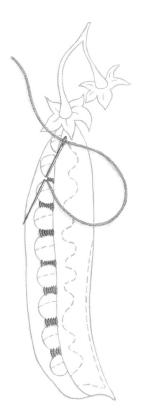

LEFT: To help clarify the shape of each pea, embroider a few satin stitches in dark green in between them. Start from the center and work outward, keeping the stitches close together, until the space between each pea has been filled.

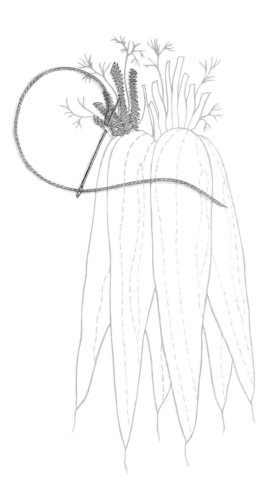

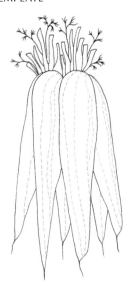

RIGHT: The carrot tops
or stems are diagonally
embroidered in dark green
satin stitch. Alter the
direction of the diagonal
with each stem.

TEMPLATE

To work the carrots

Enlarge the carrots template (see left) to 220% on a photocopier. Using dressmaker's carbon paper, transfer the design onto one corner of your cloth.

The entire design is worked with three strands of thread. For all shading, the long-and-short stitches are made horizontally across the carrot, unlike those of the peapods, which are made vertically (see photographs on pages 62 and 65). I chose to work the tops first and then the carrots, but the order is unimportant.

Using dark green, embroider the carrot tops in satin stitch diagonally across each stem (see illustration at right). Change to light green, and embroider the feathery leaves in straight stitch and their stems in stem stitch.

Embroidering the central (and only whole) carrot first, work a line of long-and-short stitches down its left side in bright orange. Moving to the right, work a line in dark orange, then medium orange, before working the area indicated by a dotted line in cream. Finish the carrot in pale orange. Embroider the two larger carrots on either side of this central carrot in the same way, but work smaller stitches to suit their narrower size. The three remaining carrots are worked in dark and pale orange only.

When all shading with long-and-short stitch is finished, outline the left-hand edge of each carrot with a line of stem stitch in the same color used for the first line of shading. Start at the top of the carrot and work downward, gradually extending the stitches to form a carrot tail (see photograph opposite). For the central carrot only, outline the right-hand side with pale orange.

COLOR GUIDE

Dark green
367

Light green
368

Bright orange
946

Dark orange
720

Medium orange
721

Cream
712

Pale orange
722

Geometrics and Initials

UNCOMPLICATED EMBROIDERY patterns are often the most effective and can turn an ordinary piece of household linen or length of fabric into something luxurious as well as personal. A curtain made from delicate lilac organza needs no more than a border of couched swirls to look magical, while a classic white napkin becomes exclusive when embroidered with an elegant initial. Geometric shapes and initials are also wonderfully versatile. They can be used singly, arranged in rows to form decorative bands (as in the Patterned Hearts project), or used at random over a large area. Different effects can be achieved simply by enlarging or reducing the motif, as well as by embroidering with different yarns. The blanket with the Sprinkled Snowflakes stitched in double knitting cotton is dramatically different from the coordinating sheet worked with fine thread,

although similar templates were used. It would be exciting to use initials in this way, stitched at random over a blanket or bedspread. Sometimes it is the surface pattern or weave of a fabric that inspires a design. The checked fabric used for the Border of Crosses tablecloth and cushion lent itself beautifully to being filled with simple embroidery stitches arranged in geometric patterns. This treatment also adds textural interest to the surface of a fabric.

LEFT: A diaphanous organza curtain is decoratively edged with cotton swirls made using couching stitch. The same pattern is reduced and applied to the contrasting tieback. OPPOSITE: An elegant H embroidered in satin stitch in a classic shade of navy blue adds a touch of luxury to a hand towel.

BORDER OF CROSSES

Both this tablecloth and cushion cover are ideal projects for the beginner, as the grid pattern of the fabric forms a guide in which to work the stitches. The crosses that form the building blocks for the two patterns are in fact double crosses, combining not only two different stitches, but also two different embroidery threads and colors. The first, and larger, diagonally formed cross is formed by four lazy-daisy stitches, while the smaller straight cross sewn on top is made from four straight stitches. Cream Pearl Cotton, a twisted thread with a sheen, alternates with stranded cotton in a contrasting color. Alternating colors and threads in this way adds extra interest to an otherwise formal design.

RIGHT: Checked fabrics offer endless possibilities for creating simple embroidery patterns. As with graph paper, the squares can be filled to form a shape or motif.

MATERIALS

- DMC Pearl Cotton No. 5 in cream 712
- DMC stranded embroidery cotton in the following colors:

    maroon 3041 (*tablecloth only*)

    green 503 (*cushion cover only*)

For the size of tablecloth worked here, allow approximately one skein of cream for three triangles and one skein of maroon for six triangles. For the cushion cover you will need two skeins each of cream and green.

For the tablecloth

- 1¾ x 2⅛yd (1.5m x 2m) of green and white checked cotton fabric with ¾in (2cm) squares (Fabric that is 56in/142cm wide will provide the 71 squares width needed, with no leeway)

For the cushion cover

- 27 x 37in (68 x 93cm) of lilac and white checked cotton fabric with ¾in (2cm) squares
- 12in (30cm) zipper
- 14in (35cm) thin foam pad

For both projects

- crewel (embroidery) needle size 5
- embroidery hoop

STITCHES USED

lazy-daisy stitch

straight stitch

For full details on stitches, see pages 132–7.

ABOVE: The squares of a checked cushion cover are filled with lazy-daisy and straight stitches to form a grid pattern.
LEFT: The same stitches are arranged on a tablecloth to create a border pattern of triangles, as well as textural interest.

TECHNIQUES

For full practical information on the methods used in this project, see pages 129–31.

To work the tablecloth

First work out the arrangement of the pattern. Lay the fabric flat on the floor. Starting on a white square near one corner, count out a width of 67 squares and a length of 91 squares. Tuck under the remaining fabric while you count out the pattern. (Of this excess, two rows of squares all around are for hemming. Do not cut the excess yet, just in case you have made a mistake with the counting.) You should now have a white square on each corner.

Count along one width edge to the center (the 34th square) and then count in four squares toward the center. Mark this square with a pin. Count 12 squares to the left and mark the 12th square with a

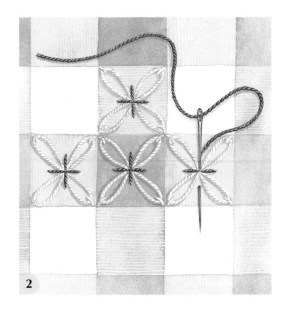

2

second pin. The 11 squares between these two pins form the bottom line of the first triangle. The triangle narrows to one square over six rows (see photograph opposite) so count up five rows from the center of the triangle base and mark the top of the triangle. Repeat once more to the left for the second triangle (leaving a dark square between each triangle) and then repeat twice on the right-hand side of the 34th square. You will now have four triangles marked out. Next, mark out the half triangles for the corners. These are six squares wide at their base.

Continue around the tablecloth, marking out six triangles on both lengths and four more on the other width, plus the corner triangles. The entire design is worked with six strands of thread. Start stitching at the top of each triangle, working four lazy-daisy stitches in cream in a diagonal cross in each square (see 1 left). In the center of each of these, work four small straight stitches in maroon (see 2 above).

1. In each square, work four diagonally placed lazy-daisy stitches. The small stitch holding down the loop of each lazy-daisy stitch should point toward the corner of the square.
2. When the diagonal crosses are complete, work a smaller cross in a contrasting color, using four straight stitches. These are positioned evenly between the four lazy-daisy stitches and should be of equal length.

1

When all the triangles are complete, embroider the outer border line along the second row in from the edge (see photograph on page 73). Start in the center of one edge. Work in the same stitches as for the triangles, but this time reverse the colors at each corner and at every sixth square. These reversed crosses should coincide with the middle of each triangle and the space between each triangle.

When the stitching is complete, hem the tablecloth with neat hand stitches, using the two rows of squares allowed for this. Cut off any excess fabric.

To work the cushion cover

First work out the arrangement of the grid pattern. Lay the fabric flat on a table and, starting on a colored square, count out a width of 17 squares and a height of 17 squares, leaving a margin of at least two rows of squares all around (one row for the seam and one for the decorative border). You should have a colored square in each corner. The embroidery is worked along this outer line of squares and every fourth row, thus forming a grid pattern. Work the stitches within each square as given for the tablecloth. Reverse the colors every fourth square, where the grid lines cross (see photograph opposite).

To finish the cushion cover

Cut around the embroidery, including the border of two squares all around. For the backing fabric measure two pieces of matching fabric, one piece 4¾ x 16½in (12 x 42cm), or 21 squares by six squares, and the other piece 13½ x 16½in (34 x 42cm), or 21 squares by 17 squares. Place the two pieces right sides together and, using a sewing machine or small back stitches, join along one long edge, using one row of squares as the seam allowance and leaving enough seam open in the middle for the length of the zipper. Press the seam flat. Pin, baste, then stitch the zipper into position.

With right sides facing and the zipper open, pin, baste, and machine stitch the embroidery to the backing fabric, leaving one row of squares all around as your seam allowance. Snip across the corners to avoid a bulky finish and turn the cushion cover to the right side. Press the seam well. Machine stitch all around the outside edge of the border of squares (see photograph opposite). Insert the cushion.

Cut out four cushion ties from the fabric remains, each 1½ x 18in (4 x 45cm). Fold each strip in half lengthwise, right sides together, and machine stitch along the long side and one short end. With the blunt end of a pencil, turn each tube right side out. Press. Tuck in the open end and hand stitch to close. Position the ties in pairs on the underneath of the cushion so that they can be tied around the back of the chair, then hand sew in place.

Using checked fabrics

There are many different checked fabrics on the market, from tiny gingham checks to bold grids. Woven checks are more suitable for embroidery; printed check fabrics are usually too flimsy. If you can't find the same-size check as the one used here, you can use a smaller check, although the resulting pattern will be smaller. To obtain the same scale of design, work more squares for each triangle. For a different effect altogether, use a small check and embroider each cross over several squares.

SIMPLE SWIRLS

This straightforward loop design, like an orderly and neatly repeating scribble or doodle, is ideally suited to couching. With couching stitch, the only stitch used for this design, the main embroidery thread is laid across the surface of the fabric and held in place with another—often contrasting—thread. This allows for enormous scope in mixing different threads and fabrics together as well as working bold designs. I have been able to use a thick knitting cotton with a fragile organza because, unlike the other embroidery stitches in this book, the nature of couching stitch means that the main thread does not pass in and out of the fabric.

LEFT AND OPPOSITE:
Embroidered swirls and loops add decorative detail to the edge of an exquisite organza curtain as well as embellishing a tieback made in contrasting fabric.

MATERIALS

- 1 x 1¾oz (50g) ball of double knitting cotton
- DMC stranded embroidery cotton in the following colors:
    cream 712 (*curtain only*)
    lilac 554 (*tieback only*)
    For the curtain border, allow one skein of cream for approximately 48in (120cm) of embroidery. For the tieback, one skein of each color is plenty.
- ready-made curtains or, if you wish to make your own, organza or any other sheer fabric made up as required
- 16 x 30in (40 x 75cm) of loose-woven cream cotton or linen fabric for the tieback
- masking tape
- water-soluble pen
- crewel (embroidery) needle size 6
- dressmaker's carbon paper

STITCHES USED

couching stitch

For full details on stitches, see pages 132–7.

TECHNIQUES

For full practical information on the methods used in this project, see pages 129–31.

To work the curtain border

Enlarge the template on page 79 to 280% on a photocopier. Place the copy on a flat surface, such as a table, and secure into position with masking tape.

1

Continue tracing the pattern, moving the fabric over the copy until the repeating pattern runs down the whole length of the curtain.

Start stitching, working from right to left. Bring the double knitting cotton up through the fabric at the right-hand end of the swirl line. Following the line of the pattern, hold the thread down with small vertical stitches of embroidery cotton (see 1 left). Inside each large loop work one small loose loop, held in place at its base with one or two stitches (see 2 below).

To work the curtain tieback

Measure two strips of fabric 4½ x 26in (11 x 66cm). Add a ¾in (2cm) seam allowance all around and cut out. Put one piece aside for the backing. On the tieback front mark three lines down the length of the fabric with the water-soluble pen, one line in the center and the other two on either side, 1in (2.5cm) from the edge (including the seam allowance). Enlarge the template opposite to 130% and transfer it onto the tieback, using dressmaker's carbon paper.

1. With the thread to be couched laid along the pattern line, make small, evenly spaced stitches to hold it in position. As you stitch, the couched thread should lie smoothly on the surface of the fabric, and should not be too slack or pulled so tight that it wrinkles the material.

2. When one large loop has been completed, make another, smaller loop over it. With just one or two vertical stitches, secure in place at the point where the yarn crosses both loops. The rest of the small loop is left unstitched so that it falls freely away from the fabric when the curtain is hung.

Place the curtain over this, starting at the bottom of the leading (or inside) edge if the border is intended for the right side of a window, or at the top of the leading (or inside) edge for a curtain on the left side of the window. You will be able to see the pattern through the fabric. Position the fabric so that the pattern is level with the edge and secure it to the table for a moment with tape. With a water-soluble pen, lightly trace the pattern directly onto the fabric.

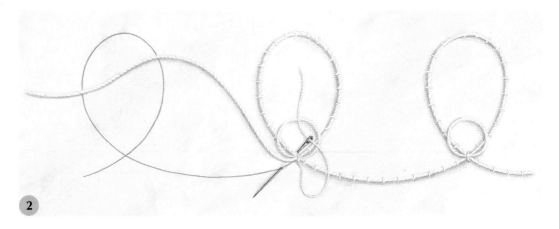

2

Keep the pattern level between the lines and reverse it on one side for a mirror effect (see photograph right). Work couching stitch along all the lines as for the curtain border, but this time use lilac embroidery cotton for the holding stitches and omit the small loose loop.

To finish the tieback

With right sides facing, place the embroidered strip over the backing. Machine stitch along the two long sides and one short end. Snip the corners diagonally to get rid of excess fabric before turning the tube to the right side. Press. Tuck in the open end and hand stitch closed.

To make the ties for the tieback, cut two strips of fabric, each 1½ x 18in (4 x 45cm). Fold each strip in half lengthwise, right sides together. Machine stitch along the long side and one short end. With the blunt end of a pencil, turn each tube right side out. Press. Tuck in each open end and hand stitch to close. Hand sew the ties onto the tieback, one at each end in the center.

TEMPLATE

COLOR GUIDE

**Cream
712**

**Lilac
554**

PATTERNED HEARTS

The heart is one of the most extensively used motifs in folk art. It has been painted on dowry chests, embroidered on cloth, and carved into furniture and over doors. Its symbolism embraces friendship, loyalty, and warmth as well as love.

   The heart designs shown here, although traditional in their use and arrangement, look modern and fresh. This is largely due to the choice of colors. There is no trace of the familiar red; instead, the colors are reminiscent of spring flowers, daffodils and lilac. While small shapes, such as petals and leaves, are ideally suited to solid stitching, larger-scale motifs, such as these hearts, look best filled with relatively open stitches or simple patterns.

RIGHT: Basic stitches, strong shapes, and the prettiest colors are combined to form a decorative band across a white honeycomb-weave towel. The pattern can be seen and fully appreciated when the towel is draped over a rail or basin.

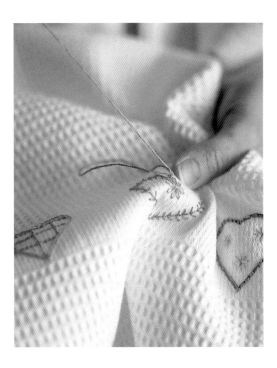

MATERIALS

- DMC stranded embroidery cotton in the following colors:
   - yellow 3821
   - lilac 340
   - green 913
   - pink 3806
   - purple 554 (*except single-motif hand towel*)

   One skein of each color is more than enough to work the embroidered shelf linen cloth with 14 hearts, as well as a repeat-motif and a single-motif hand towel.
- plain white cotton or linen fabric for shelf linen cloth (see page 82 for directions on calculating the quantity)
- length of lace trimming to fit shelf linen cloth
- cotton hand towels
- tracing paper
- crewel (embroidery) needle size 6
- dressmaker's carbon paper
- embroidery hoop

STITCHES USED

chain stitch	back stitch
straight stitch	fern stitch
lazy-daisy stitch	

For full details on stitches, see pages 132–7.

TECHNIQUES

For full practical information on the methods used in this project, refer to Techniques on pages 129–31.

ABOVE: The pattern used for the shelf linen cloth is equally effective on a hand towel. For the second hand towel, two hearts have been combined to form a different design.
LEFT: A glimpse inside a half-open cupboard reveals carefully stacked shelves covered with a cloth edged with lace and embroidered hearts.

1. For each star make eight straight stitches from the center of each dot, as marked on the template. To ensure that the stitches radiate symmetrically, work a cross first, then the diagonal stitches.

2. The outline of the fern stitch heart is worked in two halves, each starting with a back stitch.

1

2

To work the shelf linen cloth

Measure the length and width of the shelf, adding 2½in (6cm) to the width for the embroidered border and a further 1in (2.5cm) all around for the hem allowance. Mark these measurements on the cotton or linen fabric and cut out.

Trace the three different templates opposite. Using a tape measure and straight pins, plan the placement of the hearts. I positioned mine 3in (7.5cm) apart (measuring from the center of one heart to the next) and 1½in (4cm) from the bottom (including the hem allowance). Using dressmaker's carbon paper, transfer the hearts onto the fabric (see photograph on page 81 for order).

The entire design is worked with three strands of thread. Work the three different hearts as follows.

GRID HEART

The heart with the grid pattern is outlined in chain stitch in yellow. Start at the top and work around one side to the point. Repeat on the other side. Embroider the grid in lilac using back stitch.

THREE-STAR HEART

The heart with three stars is also outlined in chain stitch, this time in lilac. The yellow stars are made from eight straight stitches radiating out from a central point; this is known as Algerian Eye stitch. Bring the thread through the center of the marked dot and make one straight stitch horizontally to the left. Bring the needle up in the center again and make a second stitch, this time vertically (see 1 above). Work two more straight stitches in this way to form a cross, before working four diagonal stitches in between. Try to keep the stitches symmetrical.

FERN STITCH HEART

The third heart, worked in two color schemes, is outlined with pink or green fern stitch. Starting at the top, work one back stitch, before continuing in fern stitch around one side to the point. Repeat for the other side (see 2 above). For the star in the middle of the heart, embroider eight green or purple radiating lazy-daisy stitches, all emerging from one central point.

To finish the shelf linen cloth

When you have finished the embroidery, hem the cloth all around and add the lace trimming.

To work the repeat-motif hand towel

This is worked in exactly the same way and to the same scale as the shelf linen cloth above.

To work the single-motif hand towel

For the outer heart, enlarge the central template below to 200% on a photocopier. For the inner heart, simply trace the same template. Using dressmaker's carbon paper, transfer the hearts onto the corner of the towel. I placed mine 2in (5cm) from the side and 3in (7.5cm) from the bottom. Ensure that the smaller heart is centrally placed inside the larger heart.

The entire design is worked with three strands of thread, except for the outline of the larger heart, which is worked with six strands. Work both outlines in chain stitch, using pink for the large heart and lilac for the smaller one. Between the two outlines embroider nine yellow stars in straight stitch, and in the center work one green star in lazy-daisy stitch, as for the shelf linen cloth.

TEMPLATES

COLOR GUIDE

Yellow
3821

Lilac
340

Pink
3806

Green
913

Purple
554

ELEGANT INITIALS

During the nineteenth century it became extremely fashionable to embellish all your possessions with your initials, from crystal, china, and silverware to luggage. Even household linen did not escape the trend. Each piece was embroidered with letters taken from alphabets in a multitude of different styles from the plain and unadorned to the highly complex. Some letters were used simply for identification purposes, to enable laundry staff to distinguish one batch of white linen from another. Others were lavishly entwined to form decorative monograms and were used as embellishments, for example, in the center of grand formal tablecloths. Inspired by this tradition, the letters illustrated here will enable you to add a touch of old-fashioned elegance to your own household linen.

MATERIALS

- DMC stranded embroidery cotton in the following colors:
    - navy 336 (*hand towel only*)
    - blue 798 (*napkins only*)
  One skein is sufficient to embroider four napkins or three hand towels.
- plain cotton or linen hand towel
- plain cotton or linen napkins or, if you prefer to make your own, plain cotton or linen fabric. Allow a 20in (50cm) square of fabric for each napkin.
- crewel (embroidery) needle size 5 or 6
- dressmaker's carbon paper
- embroidery hoop

LEFT: A set of beautiful linen napkins is personalized with elegant letters embroidered in royal blue thread.
OPPOSITE: A single letter H, taken from the same alphabet on page 88 but greatly enlarged, gives an old hand towel a new lease on life.

RIGHT: When the outline shape of the letter narrows down to a single thin line, replace satin stitch with small back stitches. As soon as the line begins to thicken, return to working in satin stitch.

carbon paper, transfer the initial onto the towel, placing it near the bottom, where it will be visible when hung over a towel rail. Mount the fabric in the embroidery hoop.

The entire design is worked with three strands of thread and in satin stitch only. This is one of the most popular stitches used for embroidering letters. Work the stitches from side to side to create a solid band of color (see the cross-stroke of the A in illustration left). As the lines of the letters curl, turn the angle of the needle so that the stitches continue to lie at 90 degrees to the strokes of the letter. The stitches must not slant between these lines. Make sure that no fabric shows through between each stitch, and that all stitches lie perfectly flat on the fabric.

STITCHES USED

satin stitch

back stitch

For full details on stitches, see pages 132–7.

TECHNIQUES

For full practical information on methods used in this project, see pages 129–31. Although for many embroidery projects I think hoops are optional, they are essential for initials and monograms, where the success of the work depends on the smoothness and the closeness of the satin stitches.

To work the hand towel

Enlarge the initial of your choice from pages 88 and 89 to 245% on a photocopier. Using dressmaker's

To work the napkins

Enlarge the initial of your choice to 140% on a photocopier. Using dressmaker's carbon paper, transfer the initial onto the corner of the napkin. (Be careful not to place the initial too close to the corner or you will not be able to mount the napkin in the hoop.)

The entire design is worked with three strands of thread. Stitch most of the letter in satin stitch, working from side to side of the outline, but where the strokes of the letter are reduced to a fine line, work in very small back stitch (see illustration left). Make sure no fabric is visible between each stitch.

COLOR GUIDE

Blue
798

A B C D E F

G H I J K

L M N O P

Q R S T U

V W X Y Z

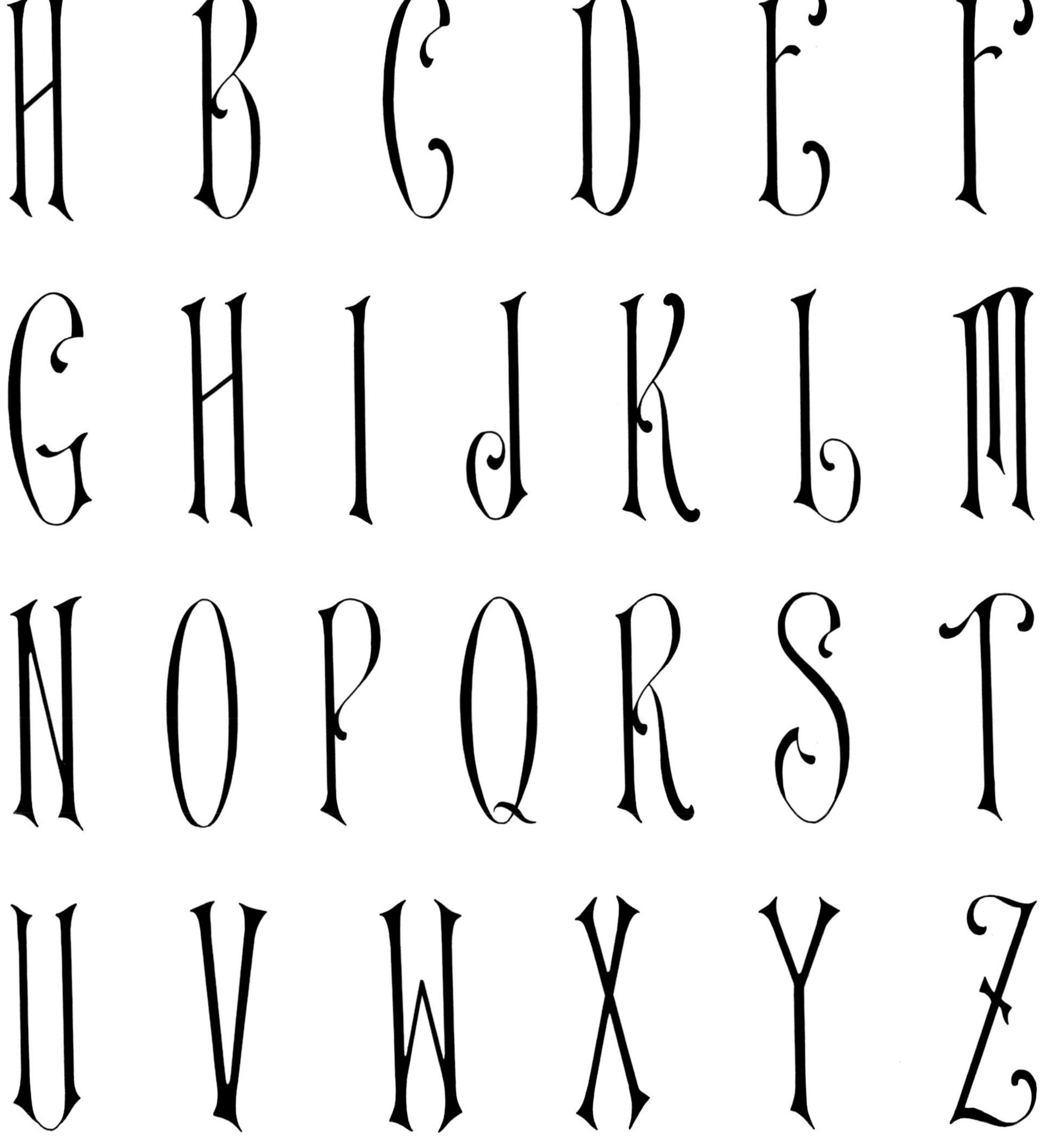

A B C D E F
G H I J K L M
N O P Q R S T
U V W X Y Z

SPRINKLED SNOWFLAKES

This snowflake project is a good illustration of how the scale of an image, and the type of embroidery thread and fabric chosen, can completely alter a design. For the main project, two different snowflakes are repeated in an orderly row along the edge of a smooth cotton sheet and daintily worked in silky yarn, using three different embroidery stitches. For the variation on the theme, a third snowflake template is dramatically enlarged and randomly scattered over a fluffy wool blanket. To complement the texture of the blanket, the snowflakes are stitched robustly in satin stitch, using cream double knitting cotton and a darning needle.

MATERIALS

- DMC stranded embroidery cotton in the following color:
    yellow 726
    Quantities used depend on the size of sheet. For a single sheet, two skeins are sufficient.
- plain cotton or linen sheet or, if you prefer to make your own, cotton sheeting or linen
- tracing paper
- crewel (embroidery) needle size 6
- dressmaker's carbon paper
- embroidery hoop

STITCHES USED

lazy-daisy stitch
back stitch
fly stitch

For full details on stitches used, see pages 132–7 .

TECHNIQUES

For full practical information on methods used in this project, see pages 129–31.

To work the sheet border

Photocopy the left- and right-hand templates on page 92, making plenty of copies. Using a tape measure and straight pins, plan their placement. I placed my larger snowflakes 8in (20cm) apart (measuring from the center of one to the other) and 1½in (4cm) from the edge of the sheet. Between these, I evenly positioned three small snowflakes. Using dressmaker's carbon paper, transfer the pattern onto the sheet.

RIGHT AND OPPOSITE:
A sprinkling of snowflakes enhances a plain cotton sheet and a wool blanket. The different scale and arrangement of snowflakes in the two designs is further emphasized by the sharply contrasting embroidery threads.

TEMPLATES

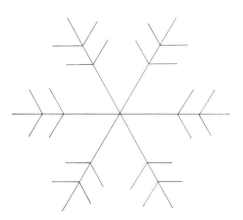

COLOR GUIDE

Yellow
726

The entire design is worked with three strands of thread. For the larger of the two snowflakes, start at one end of one of the long radiating lines. Work the tip and the four short strokes in lazy-daisy stitch. Continue down the line in back stitch to the other end, and then repeat the five lazy-daisy stitches. Repeat for the other two lines to complete the snowflake (see photograph left).

For the smaller snowflake, simply work each radiating line in fly stitch (see 1 below). Traditionally, the loop of fly stitch is secured with a small vertical stitch, but here the stitch extends to the center of the snowflake (see 2 below). Repeat both large and small snowflakes as often as required.

1. For each radiating line of the smaller snowflake, pick up a diagonal stitch, with the needle point over the loop.
2. To hold the loop in place, make a vertical stitch that extends to the center of the snowflake. Bring the needle out where the next diagonal stitch is to be worked.

1

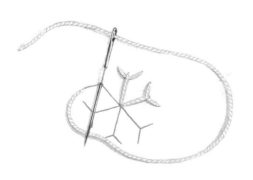

2

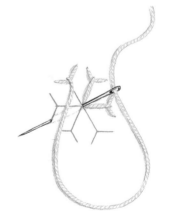

To work the design on a blanket

For a coordinating blanket, you will need to stencil the motif in place rather than use dressmaker's carbon paper, because of the fluffy nature of blanket fleece. On a photocopier, enlarge the larger snowflake template (right) to 230% and the smaller one (center, page 92) to 220%. (Make several copies for planning the placement—see below.) Paste one copy of each snowflake onto separate pieces of poster board, leaving plenty of excess board around the motifs. With a craft knife, carefully cut out the snowflakes to leave two stencils.

Plan the placement of the snowflakes using the extra copies of the motifs, then pin them temporarily in place. Lay the blanket on a smooth, flat surface and place the correct stencil in the required position. Spray the stencil very lightly with spray paint in order just to mark the snowflake on the blanket with a fine mist. Very carefully remove the stencil and allow the paint to dry thoroughly. Repeat for the required number of snowflakes.

Using a darning needle and a 1¾oz (50g) ball of double knitting cotton in cream, embroider the snowflakes in satin stitch (see photographs below and overleaf for direction of stitches).

TEMPLATE

FLORAL MONOGRAMS

The stitches that look simplest are not always the easiest to work. Satin stitch is a good example of this: to work one stitch is easy, but to work stitches in a group requires care and precision. The outer edges of a shape filled with satin stitch should be even, with each stitch lying satin-smooth over the fabric and in line with the next stitch. As a general guide, the simpler the working method of a stitch, the more practice is required for a perfect finish.

While the Elegant Initials (see page 84) show how effective satin stitch can be, these Floral Monograms are also raised with padding stitches. The light catches the curve of each raised stitch and intensifies the sheen and color of the thread.

ABOVE AND RIGHT:
The prettiest way to
personalize a linen
pillowcase or a stationery
folder is to frame your
monogram with a garland
of leaves and flowers.

MATERIALS

- DMC stranded embroidery cotton in the following colors:

    lilac 211 (*pillowcase only*)

    cream 712 (*stationery folder only*)

    Allow four skeins for the pillowcase and three for the folder, though these quantities will vary depending on the amount of padding you want.

For the pillowcase

- cotton or linen pillowcase or, if you prefer to make your own, 1¼yd (1m) of cotton sheeting or linen

For the stationery folder

- 20in (50cm) of colored cotton or linen
- two pieces of ¹⁄₁₆in (2mm) thick poster board, 10 x 14in (25 x 35cm)
- one piece of thinner poster board or heavy paper large enough to line the folder
- masking tape
- strong glue

For both projects

- crewel (embroidery) needle size 5
- dressmaker's carbon paper
- embroidery hoop

STITCHES USED

padded satin stitch

stem stitch

For full details on stitches used, see pages 132–7.

*RIGHT: To raise or pad a
letter (or any other shape),
the space within the outlines
of each letter should be
worked with rows of
running stitch. The sewing
must follow the direction of
the strokes of the letter.*

TEMPLATE

TECHNIQUES

For full practical information on methods used in
this project, see pages 129–31.

To work the pillowcase

On a photocopier, enlarge the floral template below
to 300% and the initials of your choice from pages
88 and 89 to 235%. With a pin or a couple of
basting stitches, mark the center of the pillowcase.
Using dressmaker's carbon paper, first transfer the
flowers, placing the "X" over the basting stitches to
give you the correct position. Into the center of this
floral frame, place the initials so that the bottom of
each letter is level with the basting stitches. Make
sure both the flowers and the letters are level with
the outline of the pillowcase.

The entire design is worked with three strands of
thread. First pad the flowers, leaves, and letters. Fill
the outline of each shape with rows of small running
stitches (see illustration right). The closer together the
stitches, the more raised each shape will be. Work

satin stitch over this padding, referring to the template
for the direction of the stitches. Work a single row of
stem stitch to follow each stem line.

To work the stationery folder

Cut two pieces of fabric (one for the front of the
folder and the other for the back) 16in (40cm) wide
by 12in (30cm) high. On a photocopier, enlarge the
floral template at left to 240% and the initials of
your choice from pages 88 and 89 to 185%. To
embroider the front, work as for the pillowcase.

To finish the stationery folder

Press the two fabric pieces. Sew them together along
one side edge. Press, then join the two pieces of ¹⁄₁₆in
(2mm) thick poster board along one side edge with
masking tape, taping on both sides to form a spine.
Position the hinged poster board piece open over the
back of the embroidery and the backing fabric, so
that the spine aligns with the seam. Cut the fabric

corners diagonally. Fold the overlaps, 1in (2.5cm) all around, over the poster board to the inside and tape or glue in place. Position the thinner board for the inside of the folder over the back of the hinged board to cover the fabric overlaps. Glue in place. Place under a heavy object to dry for at least an hour. On the inside of the folder, score down the center of the lining board to make a spine. Fold in half.

Home and Hearth

FLOWERS, ANIMALS, BIRDS, and simple geometric patterns are the subjects we most associate with embroidery. Equally effective, though little used, are images taken from the home. An elegant water jug, a glass perfume bottle, an old-fashioned iron, and a curvaceous wrought-iron chair are all examples of interesting shapes that can be interpreted successfully in embroidery. Because household utensils and furniture are such strong motifs, I chose to keep the embroidery at its simplest, often using stitches such as chain or stem to outline the shape and limiting myself to just one or two colors. This gives the motif the appearance of a line drawing. I find the resulting simplicity of the patterns very attractive. Different effects could be achieved by introducing more colors and stitches. Within the outline stitches, areas could be filled with lines of chain stitch placed close together for textural interest; or long-and-short stitch could be used to shade the side of a motif.

Where possible I have put the finished embroideries to practical use, or at least used them in the rooms from which the designs were gathered. Hence a shelf linen cloth decorated with a row of kettles and mugs looks wonderful on a kitchen sideboard, and a teacup is perfectly placed on a tea cozy for afternoon tea.

LEFT: The elegant curves of a wrought-iron chair find an echo in the miniature curlicue chairs embroidered onto a cushion cover.
OPPOSITE: An old-fashioned water jug and bowl in shades of blue and lilac are embroidered onto a piece of white fabric, which in turn is sewn onto a checked sink skirt. Rather than overpowering the embroidery, the contrasting fabrics act as an effective frame.

KITCHEN WARES

The naivete of the embroidered kitchen utensils is what makes these shelf borders and glass cloth so appealing. The fun of designing them lies in choosing the objects to be embroidered. Almost any kitchen utensil, as long as it has an interesting shape, can be represented with embroidery. For the shelf borders, you could add other motifs to work alongside those shown here to tell a story. Or, for a completely different look, but one that is equally striking, you could arrange the utensils informally over a tablecloth, as for the Scattered Leaves project (see page 22), and make matching napkins embroidered with one or more motifs.

ABOVE: Kitchen shelves lined with lengths of cotton fabric embroidered with water jugs, kettles, and mugs. RIGHT: An old-fashioned iron adorns the corner of a glass cloth.

MATERIALS

- DMC stranded embroidery cotton in the following colors:

    orange 350

    yellow 3821

    medium blue 798

    pale blue 799

Each of my shelf linen cloths is 44in (112cm) long and embroidered with nine utensils. To work these, two skeins of the main colors (orange and medium blue) and one of the contrasting colors would be sufficient. For one large motif on a glass cloth, one skein of each color is plenty.

- plain white cotton or linen fabric, or old sheeting with scalloped edges for the shelf linen cloth
- ready-made cotton or linen glass cloth or, if you prefer to make your own, sufficient cotton or linen fabric
- crewel (embroidery) needle size 6
- dressmaker's carbon paper
- embroidery hoop

STITCHES USED

    stem stitch (*kettle, mug and iron*)

    running stitch (*shelf border*)

    chain stitch (*water jug*)

For full details on stitches used, see pages 132–7.

TECHNIQUES

For full practical information on methods used in this project, see pages 129–31.

LEFT: In addition to outlining designs with strong colors, choosing a single image and working it in a repeat pattern also helps to emphasize the clean shapes of kitchen utensils.

RIGHT: Working in chain
stitch, first stitch the four
horizontal bands of the
water jug before starting
on the outline. Work down
one side of the jug, along
the bottom, and up the
other side. In this way, the
ends of each horizontal line
will be covered, giving
a neater finish. The
direction of the stitching
is not important.

To work the kettle and mug border

Measure out a strip of fabric to the length and width of your shelf, adding 5in (12.5cm) to the width for the embroidered border and a further 1in (2.5cm) all around for the hem allowance. Cut out.

Enlarge the kettle and mug templates below to 160% on a photocopier. Using a tape measure and straight pins, plan the placement of the utensils, alternating the kettle and mug. To help me position my motifs so that their bases were all level, I basted a line of running stitches in contrasting thread 2in (5cm) from the bottom edge of the fabric. Transfer the motifs onto the border with dressmaker's carbon paper, using the stitched line for placement.

The entire design is worked in stem stitch with three strands of thread. The outline of the kettle and the base of its lid are in orange, and the decorative banding is yellow. The mug has a yellow outline and an orange stripe.

When the embroidery is complete, remove any basting stitches. Hand sew a 1in (2.5cm) hem all around. Work a row of running stitches in orange along the bottom edge, using three threads.

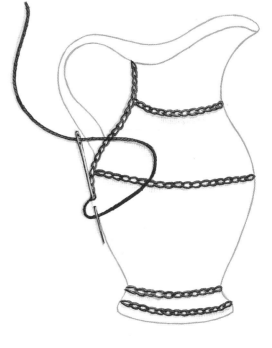

To work the water jug border

If you do not have a piece of fabric or old sheeting with a scalloped edge, work with a straight edge as for the previous border. Enlarge the jug template opposite to 185% on a photocopier. Use three

TEMPLATES

strands of thread, as for the kettle and mug border, but embroider in chain stitch rather than stem stitch, using either orange or medium blue for the outline and banding (refer to the caption on page 106 for the order of work). When the jugs are complete, work a line of chain stitch in either yellow or pale blue between each motif.

To work the glass cloth

Enlarge the utensil of your choice (I have used an iron, for which the template is provided below) to 180% on a photocopier. Using dressmaker's carbon paper, transfer the design onto the cloth, placing it across one of the corners (see photograph on page 104) where it will be visible when hung over a rack. Be careful not to place the motif too near the cloth edge, or you will not be able to mount the fabric into the hoop. The entire design is worked in stem stitch with four strands of thread (refer to the photograph for the use of color). First, work the iron base, starting with the three horizontal lines and then the outline. Next, work the sides of the handle before completing the top part.

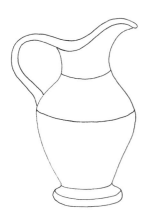

COLOR GUIDE

Orange
350

Yellow
3821

CURLICUE CHAIRS

This project was inspired by the elegant forms of wrought-iron chairs, with their elaborate curls, lattice seats, and numerous variations in style. The chairs on the cushion cover are embroidered in couching stitch using double knitting cotton, rather than fine embroidery cotton, as the surface thread. The thickness of yarn gives a raised, almost three-dimensional effect, which successfully replicates the roundness of the wrought-iron tubing.

In contrast, the chairs on the curtain tieback are worked in chain stitch, which results in the embroidery having a flatter appearance. Both the tieback and the cushion are fringed, which gives an element of fun as well as textural interest.

BELOW: A row of chairs stitched in chain stitch with cream thread decorates a pale green tieback. OPPOSITE: The chairs look equally elegant on a pale blue cushion, placed on a wrought-iron chair that mirrors the designs.

MATERIALS

- DMC stranded embroidery cotton in the following color:

    cream 712

    For the cushion cover allow one skein and for the tieback two skeins.

For the cushion cover

- 1 x 1¾oz (50g) ball of double knitting cotton
- 20 x 40in (50cm x 1m) of colored linen or cotton. This should be of sufficiently loose weave to allow the double knitting cotton to pass through easily without distorting the fabric.
- 14in (35cm) zipper
- 16in (40cm) cushion pad
- 2¼yd (2m) of fringe

For the tieback

- 10in (25cm) of colored linen or cotton
- 1¾yd (1.5m) of fringe
- 20in (50cm) of 1in (2.5cm) wide cotton tape for ties

For both projects

- triangle
- crewel (embroidery) needle size 6
- dressmaker's carbon paper
- embroidery hoop

STITCHES USED

French knot
back stitch
couching stitch (*cushion cover only*)
chain stitch (*tieback only*)
For full details on stitches, see pages 132–7.

TECHNIQUES

For full practical information on the methods used in this project, see pages 129–31.

To work the cushion cover

Using a triangle and a ruler, measure a rectangle 16 x 16½in (40 x 42cm). Add a 1in (2.5cm) seam allowance all around and cut out. Enlarge each of the three chair motifs on pages 112 and 113 twice to 190% on a photocopier. Using dressmaker's carbon paper, transfer the chairs onto the fabric, arranging them in two rows 2in (5cm) apart vertically, measuring from the base of the chairs in the

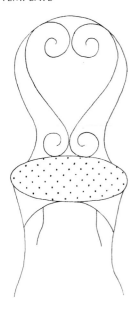

top row to the top of the chairs in the lower row, and 5in (13cm) apart horizontally, measuring from the center of one chair to the next.

Work the chair seats first. For the chair motif with the dotted seat, work one French knot for each dot, using six strands of thread. For the chair with the lattice seat and back, work the grid pattern in back stitch, using four strands of thread. For the third style of chair, work the lattice seat also in back stitch but with six strands of thread (see 1 below).

Work the rest of each chair in couching stitch. Bring the double knitting cotton up through the fabric at the beginning of a swirl, a line, or a shape. Following the line of the pattern, hold the thread down with small vertical stitches, using three strands of embroidery cotton. For a very curved shape, for example the swirls on the chair backs, the stitches should be worked closer together than for those along a straighter line, to create smoother lines (see

2 below). At the end of each line, take both the threads back to the wrong side. For circular shapes, this will also be the starting point.

To finish the cushion cover

For the backing fabric you will need to measure two pieces of fabric, one piece 4 x 16in (10 x 40cm) and the other 12¼ x 16in (32 x 40cm). Add a 1in (2.5cm) seam allowance all around and cut out. Place the two pieces right sides together, and using a sewing machine or small back stitches, join along one long edge, leaving enough seam open in the middle for the length of the zipper. Press the seams flat. Pin, baste, and then stitch the zipper into position. With right sides facing and the zipper open, pin and baste the backing fabric to the embroidery, placing the fringe between the two layers. Machine sew all around, leaving a 1in (2.5cm) seam allowance. Snip across the corners and turn

1. Work the grid pattern of each chair seat in back stitch. The needle is brought up and down only at the points where the grid lines cross.
2. To achieve a good curl, the couched thread should be stitched down more frequently along the curves of the design than along the straight lines.

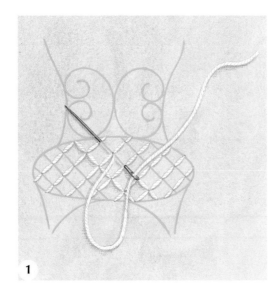

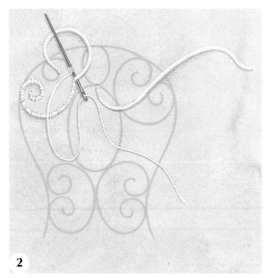

the cushion cover right side out. Press. Trim the fringe down to the required length, if necessary.

To work the curtain tieback

Measure two strips of fabric 5 x 22½in (13 x 57cm). Add a 1in (2.5cm) seam allowance all around and cut out. Put one piece aside for the backing.

Enlarge the chair templates on page 112 and below to 135% on a photocopier. You will need eight chairs. Place these in a line along the length of the fabric 3in (7.5cm) apart, measuring from the center of one chair to the next. The baseline should measure 1½in (4cm) from the edge of the fabric, including the seam allowance.

All the chairs are worked with four strands of embroidery thread. Start stitching, working the chair seats first as directed above for the cushion cover. Complete the chairs in chain stitch rather than couching stitch, and work a short row of six or seven chain stitches in between each chair and a line of chain stitch just under the chairs.

To finish the tieback

With right sides facing, pin and baste the embroidery to the backing, placing the fringe between the two layers, pointing inward. Machine sew along the two long sides and one short end. Snip the corners diagonally to get rid of excess fabric, then turn to right side. Press. Tuck in the open end, and stitch closed.

To make the ties, cut the tape into two equal pieces and fold each strip in half lengthwise, tucking in the ends. Machine stitch all around, as near to the edge as possible. Hand sew the ties onto the tieback, one at each end in the center.

COLOR GUIDE

**Cream
712**

TEMPLATES

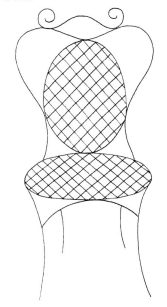

BATHTIME

Although there are many similarities between this project and Kitchen Wares (see page 104)—for example, the simple outlining of objects, the choice of stitches, and restrained color schemes—the approach to the layout and the application of the designs onto fabric is quite different. These motifs are not applied directly onto the checked fabric but instead are first embroidered onto small pieces of white fabric. These are then cut and sewn onto the sink skirt or bag, much as you would sew patchwork pieces onto a quilt. The lilac running stitch that holds the pieces in place acts as a frame for each image. For the sink skirt the designs are arranged in a loose, informal way, with no trace of a repeating pattern.

RIGHT: A gingham draw-string bag makes the perfect base on which to sew a large patchwork piece embroidered with an old-fashioned jug and bowl. OPPOSITE: The same motif, this time reduced, is combined with designs of other bathroom accessories to decorate a sink skirt.

MATERIALS

- DMC stranded embroidery cotton in the following colors:
  pale blue 809
  lilac 340
  medium blue 3807

For the draw-string bag, one skein of each color is plenty. For the sink skirt, quantities will depend on the number of patchwork pieces embroidered. I used eight motifs on mine, for which two skeins each of medium blue and lilac and one skein of pale blue sufficed.

For the sink skirt

- checked fabric measuring one-and-a-half times the width of the sink (or area to be covered) by the distance from the sink to the floor. Add a 3in (7.5cm) hem and heading allowance to the length; 2in (5cm) to the width for side hems.
- hanging wire from which to suspend the skirt, to the width of the sink (or area to be covered)

For the draw-string bag

- 27½ x 31½in (70 x 80cm) of checked fabric
- 30in (75cm) of cord

For both projects

- white cotton sheeting, enough to create as many patchwork pieces as required. In order to achieve a satisfactory result, the fabric should be of the same weight and thickness as the fabric onto which the pieces will be sewn.

- triangle
- crewel (embroidery) needle size 6
- dressmaker's carbon paper
- embroidery hoop

STITCHES USED

stem stitch
French knot (*sink skirt only*)
back stitch (*sink skirt only*)
straight stitch (*draw-string bag only*)
running stitch
For full details on stitches see pages 132–7.

TECHNIQUES

For full practical information on methods used in this project, see pages 129–131.

To work the sink skirt

On a photocopier, enlarge the mirror and hairbrush templates (left) to 180% and the perfume bottle and jug-and-bowl templates to 130%. Using dressmaker's carbon paper, transfer the designs onto the sheeting. The number of times you transfer each design will depend on the number of patchwork pieces you require. For a larger skirt or area of fabric, either transfer more motifs than the eight I used, at roughly the same distance apart, or enlarge the motifs, thus giving bigger patchwork pieces. When transferring the motifs, be sure to leave enough space around each one to allow for cutting out and hemming the patchwork pieces.

All the motifs are worked with three strands of thread. Referring to the photographs for the use of color, work each motif as follows.

WATER JUG AND BOWL

Start by stitching the diamond pattern, outlining the diamonds with stem stitch in pale blue (see 1 right). In the center of each of these diamonds outline each smaller diamond with four back stitches in lilac. For the dotted rows, embroider French knots. Working in stem stitch only, embroider the double horizontal rows above and below the diamond pattern, before outlining the whole motif in medium blue. Note that the part of the outline marking the back of the jug rim is worked in lilac for contrast. The direction of the stitches is unimportant.

PERFUME BOTTLE

The perfume bottle motif is worked entirely in stem stitch. Start by stitching the glass detail in pale blue and lilac, working all the vertical lines first. When all the inner detail is complete, embroider the outline of the bottle in medium blue thread.

HAIRBRUSH

The motif is worked entirely in stem stitch. Work the bristles of the brush first in pale blue—the direction of the stitches is unimportant—followed by the outline of the brush in medium blue. Next work a second row of stem stitch in lilac along the near edge for shading, before completing the inner detail.

MIRROR

The motif is worked entirely in stem stitch. Start by stitching the whole outline in medium blue and the two inner oval shapes in medium blue and pale blue. Where indicated by the thicker lines of the template, embroider a second row of stitches inside the outline in lilac, as close to it as possible, for shading. Finish by making two more rows of stitches between the two oval shapes in lilac.

LEFT: To outline the diamond pattern of the water jug, first work stem stitch in a continuous zig-zag line, as shown, from one side of the jug to the other. Turn and work back toward where you started. At the point where this second line crosses the first, simply stitch over the top of the first line.

1

RIGHT: A simple row of running stitches is all that is needed to sew the embroidered patchwork pieces onto the main fabric.

With a ruler and triangle, measure a square or rectangle around each motif, making sure the embroidery is centered within it. The size of each piece depends on the size of each motif as well as on the size of your skirt and the scale of the checked

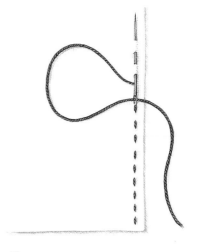

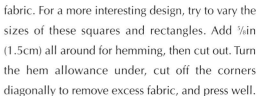

fabric. For a more interesting design, try to vary the sizes of these squares and rectangles. Add ⅝in (1.5cm) all around for hemming, then cut out. Turn the hem allowance under, cut off the corners diagonally to remove excess fabric, and press well.

To finish the sink skirt

Turn under a double ½in (12mm) hem at the two side edges. Turn over the top edge by 1½in (4cm) and machine stitch two lines of stitching (one ¼in/6mm and the other 1in/2.5cm from the top) to form a channel for the hanging wire. Turn under and stitch a 1½in (4cm) hem on the lower edge of the skirt.

Lay the skirt flat on the floor and randomly arrange the embroidered pieces on it. When you are satisfied with their arrangement, pin and baste them into position. Using three strands of lilac embroidery thread, secure the pieces all around with a row of running stitches (see 2 above).

To work the draw-string bag

Enlarge the jug and bowl template on page 116 to 210% on a photocopier. Transfer the design onto the sheeting with dressmaker's carbon paper.

Unless stated otherwise, the motif is worked with six strands of thread. As for the jug and bowl motif described on page 117, start by stitching the diamond pattern in stem stitch, using three strands of thread in pale blue and lilac. This time, however, work the inner diamonds in stem stitch rather than back stitch, and replace the French knots with tiny crosses (see photograph right), formed from two straight stitches, one diagonally over the other. Work the banding lines in stem stitch in lilac then outline the jug and bowl in stem stitch with medium blue thread, using lilac for the back of the jug rim.

With a ruler and triangle measure a rectangle 8 x 8½in (20 x 22cm) around the design. Make sure the design is centered. Add a ⅝in (1.5cm) hem allowance all around, then cut out. Turn this under, cutting the corners diagonally, and press.

To finish the draw-string bag

Cut out two pieces of checked fabric 14 x 25in (35 x 63cm), adding a ¾in (2cm) seam allowance all around. Position the embroidery on the front of one piece, 3in (7.5cm) from the lower edge (excluding the seam allowance). Pin and baste. Using three strands of medium blue thread, secure all around with a row of running stitches (see 2 opposite), making sure the stitches are evenly spaced and even in length.

With right sides facing, sew the back and front pieces together along the side and lower edges with ¾in (2cm) seams, leaving a 2in (5cm) opening on

one side for the cord, approximately 4¾in (12cm) from the top. Turn under a ¾in (2cm) hem on the top edge. Turn the bag to the right side and fold over the top to the inside so that the fold line falls mid-way along the opening. Stitch a 1in (2.5cm) channel along the top edge to hold the cord. The stitching line will pass just under the opening for the cord. Thread the cord through the channel and knot the ends together.

COLOR GUIDE

Pale blue
809

Lilac
340

Medium blue
3807

AFTERNOON TEA

Part of the fun of embroidery is that it is so easy to alter a design; you can create very different effects simply by varying the stitches. A cup and saucer outlined in back stitch and chain stitch with lazy-daisy flowers has a more delicate appearance than a cup and saucer boldly embroidered with long-and-short stitch. The floral cup-and-saucer design also has more detail, and so lends itself well to being enlarged. Areas of solid stitch work best in smaller shapes.

OPPOSITE: For the table mat, the flowers on the teacup are replaced with solid bands of long-and-short stitch. BELOW: The tea cozy makes a beautiful frame for the cup and saucer motif.

MATERIALS

- DMC stranded cotton in the following colors:

  For the tea cozy
    medium pink 335
    paler pink 962
    plum 3802
    yellow 3822
    green 3348

  For the table mat
    medium pink 335
    green 3348
  One skein of each color is plenty for both projects.

For the tea cozy
- 16in (40cm) of cream cotton or linen
- 20in (50cm) of thinner white or cream cotton fabric for lining
- 20in (50cm) square of batting
- brown paper for making tea cozy pattern
- tailor's chalk

For the table mat
- 20in (50cm) square of medium to heavy cream cotton or linen

For both projects
- triangle
- tracing paper
- crewel (embroidery) needle size 6
- dressmaker's carbon paper
- embroidery hoop

STITCHES USED

For the tea cozy
    lazy-daisy stitch
    French knot
    straight stitch
    chain stitch
    back stitch

For the table mat
    long-and-short stitch
    stem stitch
    chevron stitch
For full details on stitches, see pages 132–7.

TECHNIQUES

For full information, see pages 129–31.

To work the tea cozy

First measure on paper a squared-off version of your tea cozy shape, using the size of your teapot as a guide. Cut out your rectangle and fold it in half

lengthwise. Starting from the bottom corner away from the fold, draw a freehand curved line up and over to the top of the fold. When you are happy with the shape, cut it out and unfold the paper to give the full tea cozy shape. Using this template, draw two tea cozy shapes on the cotton or linen with tailor's chalk. Add a 1in (2.5cm) seam allowance all around and cut out. Put one piece aside for the backing.

Enlarge the teacup template below to the size of your choice on a photocopier. Using dressmaker's carbon paper, transfer the design onto the center of the tea cozy.

The entire design is worked with six strands of thread. Work the floral pattern first, referring to the photographs for the use of color. Each flower head is made up of six lazy-daisy stitches (or four where only part of the flower is visible) radiating evenly from its center. Into the center of each, work one French knot. The crosses between each flower are made with four straight stitches. Except for the outer rim of the cup and saucer, which are worked in chain stitch, the remaining outline is in back stitch.

TEMPLATE

COLOR GUIDE

Medium pink	Paler pink	Plum	Yellow	Green
335	962	3802	3822	3348

To finish the tea cozy

Place the embroidered and backing fabric pieces right sides together and, using a sewing machine or small back stitches, join along the curved edge. Hem both sides of the bottom edge and turn the cozy right side out. Press.

Use the paper template to measure four tea cozy shapes on the lining fabric. Add a 1in (2.5cm) hemming allowance along the bottom, and cut out. Measure two pieces of batting to match, but do not add any seam or hem allowances. Cut out. With right sides of one pair of linings together, pin, baste, and machine sew a ⅝in (1.5cm) seam along the curve. Repeat for the other pair. Turn one of the linings right side out and put the second inside it.

Assemble the under-cozy by pushing the two pieces of batting in between the lining layers. Turn in the bottom edges of both linings and hand sew together. To keep the batting in position, hand sew a few random stitches right through the lining and the batting. For each stitch, oversew a few times in each place and finish off before starting the next stitch. The thread should not pass from one stitch to the other. When the batting is attached, slip the padded under-cozy inside the embroidered cozy.

To work the table mat

Using a triangle and ruler, measure a rectangle 10 x 14in (25 x 35cm). Add a 1½in (4cm) hem allowance all around and cut out. Press this hem under while working out the placement of the cups and chevron lines.

Trace or photocopy the cup template opposite and transfer it onto each of the table mat corners (see

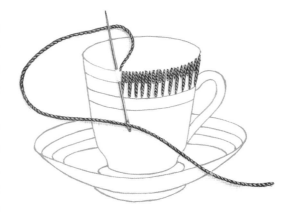

LEFT: The two extra lines added around the rims of the cup and saucer are simply guidelines for the length of the stitches. Working either from top to bottom or bottom to top, alternate with long and short stitches, as shown, keeping the outer edge of the rim level.

photograph on page 121) using dressmaker's carbon paper. Remember when tracing and transferring the design not to include the flower pattern; instead replace it with two extra lines (see illustration above).

The entire design is worked with four strands of thread. Work the solid areas of color first in long-and-short stitch. Embroider around the top edge of the cup, using the first line below the rim as a guide for the length of the short stitches, and the next line as a guide for the long stitches (see illustration above). When one row of long-and-short stitches has been completed, work a second row below this first row, embroidering short stitches below long, and long stitches below short. Repeat for the saucer.

Complete the cups and saucers by working all outlines in stem stitch. Embroider a line of chevron stitch between each cup, 1¼in (3cm) from the mat edge (see photograph on page 121). To help keep the chevron stitches even, first work a row of running stitches along the line to be embroidered. Remove this guideline when the embroidery is complete. Hem the table mat with neat hand stitches.

Techniques and Stitches

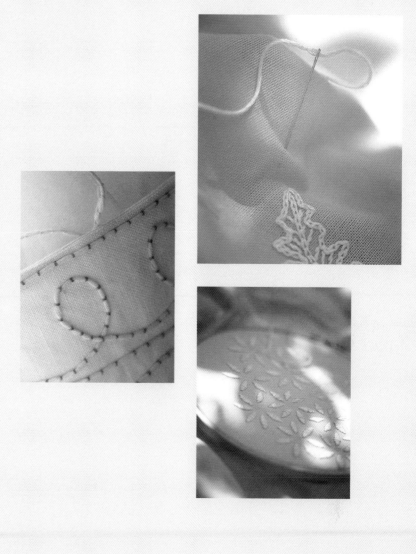

FABRICS FOR EMBROIDERY

Apart from very loosely woven fabrics, almost any fabric can be used for embroidery. However, the choice of fabric will be largely dictated by the use of the finished item. For items that will be washed frequently, such as an embroidered tablecloth or hand towel, linen is an ideal choice. This strong fabric launders well, looking fresh time and time again, and with no distortion of the design. Always prewash fabric if the item will have to be laundered, so that any shrinkage occurs at this stage.

Other factors to consider when choosing fabric are the style of the design and the yarn. A design with fine outlines and delicate details to be embroidered in a stranded silk requires a smooth-surfaced and closely woven fabric. A simpler, bolder design using thicker thread works best on a heavier, even-textured, and more loosely woven fabric. The looseness of weave will allow the thickness of the needle and thread to pass smoothly through the fabric without leaving holes showing.

Nearly all the projects in this book were made using linen and cotton. Both these fabrics are known as even-weave fabrics, which means they have an equal number of threads (warp and weft) in each direction. This evenness of weave minimizes distortion and pulling during stitching, which makes these fabrics ideal for embroidery, particularly where dense stitching occurs.

Linen and cotton are both widely available, and also come in many different thicknesses, textures, and colors.

EMBROIDERY THREADS

Just as almost any fabric can be used for embroidery, so too can most threads, from silks, cottons, and linens to wools—even string. Whichever thread you choose, it is essential that it fits the design. Stitches worked in different threads or thicknesses of thread will take on a very different appearance. A line of stem stitch worked in silk looks delicate, while the same stitch in a thicker, twisted thread is bolder and more dramatic. For this reason stranded cotton is the most commonly used embroidery thread. It is made up of six fine strands

that can be separated to create different thicknesses of thread and used on any type of fabric. Stranded cotton comes in an enormous selection of colors and is widely available. Because of its versatility and wonderful silky sheen (which have earned it its other name—embroidery silk), I chose to use it for the majority of the projects in this book.

The other cotton embroidery thread I have used is Pearl Cotton. This is a slightly twisted thread and is the most satiny of the embroidery threads. The strands cannot be separated but it is available in several thicknesses (or "gauges")—3, 5, 8 and 12, of which 3 is the thickest.

When buying thread for the projects in this book, remember that the amounts given are only approximate and will vary from one person to another, depending on how close together the stitches are worked, how much thread is used in starting and finishing, and the tension of the stitching. If you wish to duplicate my embroidery designs exactly, buy the same color, brand, and weight of embroidery thread as recommended in the "Materials" list. If you wish to substitute threads of another brand, refer to the conversion chart on page 143 or, better still, experiment with different threads and colors. By trying out ideas on a spare piece of fabric you will soon learn how different threads, fabrics, and stitches work together.

NEEDLES

The importance of using the right needle for embroidery cannot be overemphasized. The most common needle for embroidery is a crewel needle. It has a sharp point to pierce the fabric with ease and a long, slender eye. These needles are available in a range of sizes from 1 to 10; the lower the number, the larger the needle. It is important that the eye of the needle be sufficiently large to allow the thread to pass through easily without fraying. However, the threaded needle must not be too thick to pass through the fabric. If a needle leaves large holes in a fabric, use a finer one.

In time all needles will start to loose their shiny plating. When this happens, and the needle feels a little sticky and appears tarnished, change it for a new one.

FRAMES

Everyone should work embroidery in the way that she or he feels most comfortable. There are no hard and fast rules about using frames for embroidery. Some people prefer to use a frame, which holds the fabric taut, while others find it easier to work the fabric in their hands.

The most commonly used frame for embroidery is a hoop frame. These are available in all sizes, but the basic design is the same, consisting of two wooden hoops that fit one inside the other. The fabric (at the area where you will be working) is laid over the smaller hoop and the larger hoop is placed over the top. This pulls the fabric taut and even. A screw on the larger hoop adjusts the tension to keep the fabric stretched. For large pieces of embroidery where a design is too big to fit into the area of the hoop, the hoop can be moved around. It is important to remove the hoop in between periods of work, otherwise it can stretch the fabric permanently and leave unsightly marks.

Because there are many types of frames to choose from, my advice would be to visit your local needlework store where the staff will advise you on which type of frame, if any, is most suitable for you.

ADDITIONAL EQUIPMENT

In addition to needles and frames, very few tools are required for successful embroidery. A pair of small, very sharp pointed embroidery scissors are essential, as well as a larger pair for cutting fabric. For transferring patterns onto fabric you will need tracing paper and dressmaker's carbon or transfer paper. The latter is a nonsmudge carbon paper that is available in several colors. Make sure you choose a color that contrasts well with the color of your fabric, so that the working lines are clearly visible. For marking fine details directly onto the fabric, use a water-soluble marking pen. And last, but perhaps most important, a good light source is essential.

TRANSFERRING THE PATTERN

After choosing the design you wish to embroider and gathering your materials, the next stage is to transfer the design onto the fabric. Each project in this book includes a template or line drawing of the design(s). In some cases these templates are actual size and all you need to do is trace the pattern using tracing paper. Other templates have been reduced in scale to fit into the format of the book, and it is necessary to enlarge them on a photocopier. Wherever this is required, the relevant percentages are provided.

The simplest way to transfer a design onto fabric is to use dressmaker's carbon paper, and this is the method I have used throughout this book. Note that before you start any stitching, it is important to transfer the whole design. This point cannot be overemphasized, particularly when you are working repeat patterns that join up (see pages 18–21), because once stitching has started, it is very difficult to line up a pattern successfully.

Before transferring the design onto the fabric, press the fabric so that it is completely smooth. Place the fabric right side up on a flat, hard surface and, if necessary, hold it in position with masking tape. Place the carbon paper, shiny side down, on the fabric, and use tape to secure it. Place the traced or photocopied design on top of the carbon paper and tape it in position.

Pressing hard, trace carefully over the pattern with a fine ballpoint pen. If you press too lightly, the carbon paper lines will be not only too faint to work with, but also more likely to brush off before the embroidery is complete. Be especially careful not to lean on the carbon paper, because it does have a tendency to smudge. When the tracing is complete, carefully remove both the carbon and pattern papers. The fabric is now ready to embroider.

When working your embroidery, try to make sure that the stitches cover the carbon paper lines fully, so that no carbon shows when the embroidery is complete. If any lines do show, however, a quick wash will easily remove them.

Sometimes I like to work a design or detail of a pattern directly onto the fabric, thus bypassing the use of carbon paper. For this I use a water-soluble pen. Do not use a pencil, as the lead will only dirty the embroidery thread.

STARTING AND FINISHING WORK

An embroidery thread should be cut no longer than 20in (50cm). Longer lengths are more difficult to work with because they have a tendency to twist and knot. When starting to work, leave a 1in (2.5cm) loose end at the back of the fabric and catch it down with the first few stitches. Knots should always be avoided in embroidery. When finishing off, the end of the thread should be run through the back of the last few stitches on the wrong side. Once the thread has been secured in this way, you can cut off any excess.

Where you start to stitch is, I think, largely a matter of personal preference. I prefer to work the outline of a motif first and then fill in the center. If you make a mistake during stitching, take extra care when unpicking the stitches, otherwise you risk damaging the fabric. Carefully snip each wrong stitch with a pair of small, sharp pointed scissors and gently pull out the cut ends, using tweezers if necessary.

WASHING EMBROIDERY

Embroidery is best washed in plenty of hot water and mild detergent. If the ends have been started and finished properly, if the fabric has been preshrunk and the colors are fast, there is nothing to fear. I even put my large pieces of embroidery into the washing machine, although I am careful not to overspin.

Do not tumble dry embroidery; instead, gently straighten it out and hang it up to dry. While the embroidery is still damp, press it on the wrong side. To avoid flattening the stitches when pressing, place a thick towel or an old sheet folded several times over the ironing board and place the embroidery on top. If the embroidery is too dry, place a damp cloth over the work before starting to press.

Stitches

The embroidery stitches described and illustrated here are some of the most elementary and frequently used, and they are all you will need to complete the projects in this book. Each one can be applied to any design, whether floral, geometric or pictorial, and can be worked with all types of embroidery silks, cottons, stranded cottons or embroidery wools.

BACK STITCH

While running stitch (see page 136) produces a broken line of stitches, back stitch makes a more solid line. If the stitches are kept very small, back stitch can outline any shape, however awkward, which makes it ideal for embroidering fine details such as tiny stems and leaf tendrils.

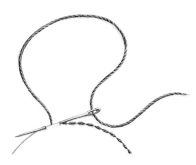

To work

Working from right to left, bring the needle up through to the right side of the fabric and make a short backwards stitch along the working line. With the needle now at the back of the work, take a long stitch forward and bring the needle up to the left of the backward stitch. The long stitch should be twice the length of the backward stitch. Take another short backward stitch on top, joining with the last stitch, and repeat in this way for the required distance. The stitches on top should be equal in length, with no gaps left between them.

BLANKET STITCH

Blanket stitch is frequently used along the edges of household linens and blankets (hence the name) to add a decorative and colourful trim, as well as to secure raw edges. By varying the length and angle of the stitches, numerous different decorative effects can be achieved.

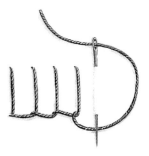

To work

Blanket stitch is worked between parallel lines with the stitches all one length. Working from left to right, bring the thread through on the bottom line and hold it down with the left thumb. Insert the needle to the right on the top line and bring it out on the bottom line immediately below, with the point of the needle over the held thread, i.e. the loop. Pull the needle through until the thread lies flat on the material with the loop pulled tight. Continue working towards the right. When the stitches are worked closely together, this is called buttonhole stitch.

CHAIN STITCH

Chain stitch is made by working a series of single looped stitches together in a line, with each stitch linking into the loop of the previous one. It is a very neat and simple stitch and is particularly effective as an outline stitch (see pages 30–5).

To work

Bring the needle through at the point where the first stitch is to be and hold the thread down towards you with the left thumb. Insert the needle in again just to the right of where the thread first emerged, then take a downwards stitch of the required length. Pass the thread under the point of the needle and pull the needle through until the loop lies flat. Hold the thread down and again insert the needle just to the right of the emerging thread and inside the loop already made. Work a stitch of the same length as the previous one, and continue the chain in this way.

CHEVRON STITCH

Chevron stitch is worked between two parallel lines and from left to right. It is most frequently used as a border stitch, but also works well as a filling stitch when it is embroidered in rows.

To work

1. Beginning at the left-hand end of the lower line, make a back stitch (see page 132), with the needle emerging for the second stitch half-way along this stitch.
2. Working to the right, take the needle to the top line and, with it pointing to the left, make a small stitch.
3. Make a back stitch to the right along the top line, emerging again half-way back along the stitch.
4. Take the needle back down to the bottom line and form the bottom stitch in the same way as shown for the top stitch in steps 2 and 3. Continue in this way, alternating between the bottom and top lines to create a zig-zag effect.

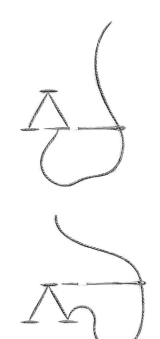

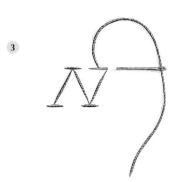

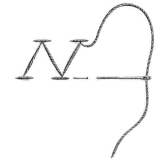

COUCHING STITCH

When loose threads are stitched down with another thread, this is known as couching. There are many ways in which the threads can be held in place, but for the purpose of this book I have worked couching stitch only in its simplest form (see pages 76–79).

FERN STITCH

Fern stitch is made up of three straight stitches radiating from a central line. All three stitches should be equal, but their size depends on the design. It is useful for delicate, fernlike sprays (see pages 18–21) and for the veins of leaves.

To work

1. Mark the length of one stitch down the central working line and bring the needle through at the bottom point of the stitch. Work one straight stitch to the right, at a 45-degree angle to the central line, and then point the needle back toward the left, and bring it out at the top of the central working line.

2. Make a stitch down the central line, inserting the needle at the bottom of the first stitch. Make one straight stitch to the left, similar in length and angle to the one on the right.

3. Pull the needle through, and take it back to the central line, inserting it where the first and second stitches meet. Take a stitch of the same length as the others down the central line. Continue as before for the required length.

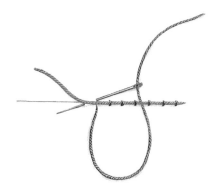

To work

Bring the thread that is to be stitched down through to the right side of the fabric and lay it along the line to be worked. Hold securely in place with the left hand. With another needle and finer thread, work tiny and evenly spaced vertical stitches along the length of the first thread to keep it in place.

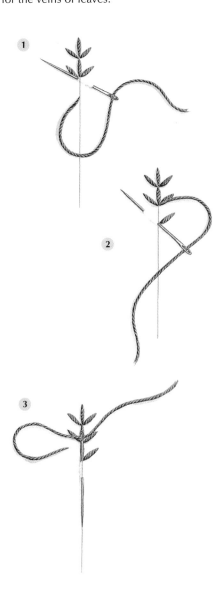

FLY STITCH

This very simple and versatile stitch can be worked in rows, groups, or as a single detached stitch.

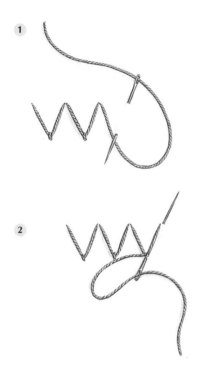

FRENCH KNOT STITCH

A French knot looks like a small bead lying on a piece of fabric. This detached stitch can be worked to form a line or a group and is often used in embroidery to give focus to the centers of flowers (see pages 36–41) and to form the eyes of tiny animals and birds.

LAZY-DAISY STITCH

Lazy-daisy is also known as detached chain stitch because each stitch stands alone. Each single chain stitch is secured at the top by a small stitch.

To work

1. Bring the needle through at the point where the top of the stitch is to be and hold the thread down toward you. Insert the needle to the right and take a diagonal stitch downward to the center. Pull the needle through, keeping the thread under the point of the needle, until a V shape is formed.
2. Insert the needle just below the thread, making a tiny vertical holding stitch. Bring the point out at the top of the next stitch.

To work

1. Bring the needle through at the point where you want the knot to be. With the left hand, hold the thread taut. Wind the thread around the needle once or twice (depending on the size of knot you want).
2. Turn the needle around and insert it into the fabric close to where the thread first emerged, still keeping the thread taut. Pull the needle through, releasing the thread at the very last minute.

To work

1. Bring the needle through at the point where the top of the first stitch is to be and hold the thread down toward you with the left thumb. Insert the needle again just to the right of where the thread first emerged, then take a downward stitch of the required length.
2. Pass the thread under the needle point and pull the needle through until the thread lies flat. Put the needle in again just beneath the loop to make a small vertical holding stitch. Repeat for each stitch.

LONG-AND-SHORT STITCH

Long-and-short stitch is used to cover large areas with thread. Only the first row consists of long and short straight stitches, the following rows being worked in even-length stitches (except where the outline restricts their size). The blended effect makes the stitch ideal for shading.

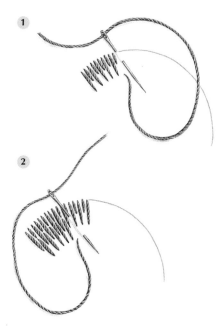

To work

1. First work a row of straight stitches, alternating long and short. Keep the outer edge of the shape even.
2. Work a row of even-length stitches into the short stitches of the first row, passing the needle through the tip of the stitch above. Continue with rows of even-length stitches until the required area is filled.

RUNNING STITCH

This stitch is identical to the running stitch used in sewing. It consists of short stitches running in and out of the fabric in a single line. It is the perfect stitch for outline work, in particular where a broken line, rather than a heavier, solid one, is required.

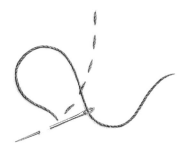

To work

Working from right to left, pass the needle in and out of the fabric to create a broken line of stitches along the line to be worked. It is important to keep the stitches and the spaces between the stitches even. The resulting effect depends not only on the size of the stitches but also on the thickness of thread used: the thicker the embroidery thread, the larger the stitch.

SATIN STITCH

Satin stitch is the most commonly used stitch for filling an area with solid color. The stitches are worked evenly from one side of the shape to the other and are so close together that no fabric shows through. Satin stitch is ideal for smaller shapes, such as petals and leaves, but less suitable for large areas, where the result can be loose and untidy. One solution for large areas is to work several rows of satin stitch, but I would usually recommend using some other filling stitch, such as long-and-short stitch.

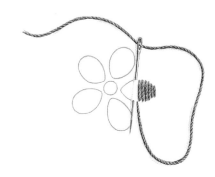

To work

Bring the needle through from the wrong side at the lower edge of the space to be filled. Insert it at the top edge and bring the needle out again at the bottom, close to the thread. The first stitch, which can be either upright or sloping, sets the angle for all following stitches. All stitches must be parallel, without overlapping, and should be smooth and neat.

PADDED SATIN STITCH

For a raised effect, the area to be covered in satin stitch is first padded. When the stitches are made, the light catches on the curves of the padding to create an extra richness and depth of color.

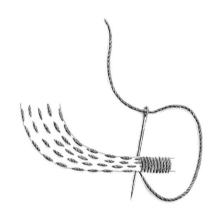

To work

First work a row of small running stitches inside the outline of the shape to be filled, then fill the area inside with further rows of running stitches. Now work satin stitch over this padding.

STEM STITCH

Stem stitch is one of the most widely used stitches in embroidery, and is sometimes known as crewel or outline stitch. The stitches slightly overlap one another to produce an unbroken and very smooth running line. This makes it particularly good for creating curves.

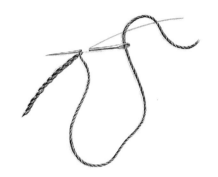

To work

Bring the needle through to the right side of the fabric, just to the left of the working line. Take the needle a little way along the working line and, with it pointing back toward the left, insert it just to the right of the line, making a stitch at a slight angle across the line. Pull the needle through and repeat, keeping the length and angle of the stitches even. The stitch can be worked with the thread to either the right or the left of the needle, but it must be consistent

Altering the angle of the stitches can vary the thickness of the line. For fine lines, pass the needle directly along the working line. For a thicker effect, pass it on either side.

STRAIGHT STITCH

Straight stitch, also known as stroke or single stitch, is simply one single, flat stitch and is the basis of many other stitches. The stitches can be grouped in many different ways to create simple shapes (see pages 70–75) or worked detached from any neighboring stitch to add detail to a design.

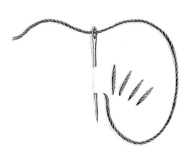

To work

Bring the needle through to the right side of the fabric and make one stitch of any length and in any direction. If several straight stitches are to be worked near one another, bring the needle out each time in the right place to make the next stitch.

Index

THE DESIGNS IN THIS BOOK were embroidered with DMC stranded embroidery cotton. If you prefer to work in Anchor embroidery cotton, refer to the conversion chart below. It lists all the DMC shades used, followed by the nearest equivalent Anchor shade available. These alternatives, however, are only approximate equivalents and will therefore give a slightly different effect from that shown in the pictures. Both DMC and Anchor threads are widely available in department stores and needlework shops. If you have problems finding a retail source near you, contact the relevant distributor listed below.

DMC - Anchor

210 - 108	**349** - 13	**503** - 875	**720** - 326	**783** - 306	**962** - 75	**3348** - 254	**3805** - 63
211 - 342	**350** - 11	**553** - 98	**721** - 324	**791** - 178	**973** - 290	**3607** - 87	**3806** - 62
304 - 19	**367** - 262	**554** - 96	**722** - 323	**798** - 131	**987** - 262	**3608** - 86	**3807** - 122
309 - 39	**368** - 261	**606** - 334	**726** - 295	**799** - 130	**988** - 261	**3687** - 76	**3819** - 278
321 - 47	**436** - 363	**666** - 46	**727** - 293	**809** - 130	**989** - 261	**3705** - 35	**3820** - 306
335 - 38	**470** - 267	**676** - 886	**729** - 890	**815** - 1005	**3041** - 871	**3746** - 110	**3821** - 305
336 - 150	**471** - 265	**704** - 256	**738** - 942	**913** - 203	**3051** - 861	**3779** - 868	**3822** - 295
340 - 1030	**472** - 254	**712** - 926	**743** - 305	**946** - 330	**3347** - 266	**3802** - 897	**3823** - 292

DMC Pearl Cotton No 5 shade **712** - Anchor Pearl Cotton shade 2

Distributors

DMC

USA AND CANADA

The DMC Corporation
Port Kearny
Building 10
South Kearny,
New Jersey 07032
Tel: 201 589 0606

ANCHOR

USA

Coats and Clarks
30 Patewood Drive
Greenville 351,
South Carolina 29615
Tel: 864 234 0331

CANADA

Coats Patons
1001 Roselawn Avenue
Toronto,
Ontario M6B 1B8
Tel: 416 782 4481

Acknowledgments

Author's THIS BOOK WOULD NOT HAVE BEEN POSSIBLE WITHOUT THE HELP AND COMMITMENT OF SUCH A WONDERFUL TEAM OF PEOPLE.

A very big thank you to Carolyn Jenkins for her beautifully precise illustrations; to Alison Bolus for her meticulous checking and rechecking of text; and to Jane Moran, Rosalind Fairman, and Marie Willey, who were so generous in allowing us to invade their homes and gardens for photography. I would also like to extend a special thanks to Tessa Clayton for her help, and to Cara Ackerman at DMC.

I am, as always, indebted to Fiona Lindsay, my agent, for her constant guidance and to Suzannah Gough for inviting me to join Conran Octopus.

In particular, I wish to thank Alison Barclay for designing such an exquisite book, and Helen Ridge for not only pulling the whole book together but for her unending support and patience. A very special thank you to Sandra Lane, who took all the glorious photographs and with whom I had such fun.

Thank you, Charles, as always, for your enormous support and constant encouragement.

Publisher's The publisher would like to thank Jane Cavolina; Andrew Whiteley – The Inkshed for the calligraphy on the jacket and chapter openers; and King & King for the alphabets on pages 88 and 89. Thanks, also, to The Blue Door, 77 Church Road, London SW13 (Tel: 0181 748 9785) for the checked fabric used in the Border of Crosses project; the wool blanket in the Sprinkled Snowflakes project; and the blue linen in the Delicate Posies project.